ASHISH SINGH comes from a very humble background from the eastern part of Uttar Pradesh. After completing college in 2007, he moved to Mumbai and began working in the IT industry. Since he had an interest in the Indian stock market and how it worked, he started reading about it.

Then, in his own words:

"Gradually, I heard about derivatives trading, started reading about it, and was completely awestruck with all the permutations and combinations it offers a trader. Since I had the cushion of a job to financially support my passion, I started trading after the 2008 market crash. Markets were in a recovery mode at that time, so buying options gave me good profits but the real lessons — read, losses — and dynamics I learnt when the markets were stagnant in 2010. Through my first book *Making Money by Selling Options — Simplified* and now this second book that is in your hands, I am sharing with you my nearly two decade-long learnings and experience of options trading."

~

Also by
Ashish Singh

~

Making Money by Selling Options — Simplified

TOP 16 OPTIONS TRADING STRATEGIES — SIMPLIFIED

Powerful Strategies for Bullish, Bearish and Sideways Markets

ASHISH SINGH

VISION BOOKS

www.visionbooksindia.com

www.visionbooksindia.com

Disclaimer

Investing and trading invariably involve some risk. The author and the publisher disclaim all legal or other responsibilities for any losses which readers may suffer by investing or trading based on information provided in this book, which is meant only for educational purpose. Readers are advised to seek professional advice and guidance before making any trades or investments.

A Vision Books Original

ISBN 10: 81-947275-5-3
ISBN 13: 978-81-947275-5-2

First Published in 2025 by
Vision Books Pvt. Ltd.
(Incorporating Orient Paperbacks and CARING imprints)
24 Feroze Gandhi Road, Lajpat Nagar 3
New Delhi 110024, India.
Phone: (+91-11) 2984 0821 / 22
e-mail: visionbooks@gmail.com

Printed at
Ashim Print Line
38/2, 35 & 36 Sahibabad Industrial Area, Ghaziabad
Uttar Pradesh 201010, India

Dedication

~

To my better half Kumud, whose continuous insistence and encouragement inspired me to write this book.

And, for our kids, Nandini and Arjun.

"Market fluctuations are chances which need to be seized wisely"

Contents

Part 1

Bullish Strategies

Part 5

Trading Options

Preface

THIS IS MY SECOND BOOK on demystifying and simplifying options trading. My earlier book, *Making Money by Selling Options — Simplified* has found widespread acceptance among readers and traders. The enthusiasm with which readers embraced it is what motivated me to write this second book, *Top 16 Options Trading Strategies — Simplified.*

There is a fundamental difference between this book and my first one. The earlier book was focused more on executing option trades based on the concept of standard deviation (SD), and the use of 1-SD strategies. The earlier book also explains how to calculate intrinsic values and payoffs for different market expiries, and how to manage trades if things go wrong.

This book, on the other hand, is designed as a ready reference to help you select appropriate option trading strategies for different market conditions. To that end, this book offers you 16 powerful and popular option strategies which you can use to trade options in bullish, bearish and sideways, i.e. range bound, market conditions. It explains each strategy fully, along with its various payoff, namely profit / loss, scenarios. It also analyses how the various Greeks impact option pricing for each strategy.

This book, thus, provides you a full toolbox of option trading strategies — and also specific guidance about how and when to use each one. Sometimes one can lose a profitable trading opportunity if you don't know which strategy to use in the prevailing market situation. This book solves such issues and confusion. Whichever direction the market may be heading for, or wherever you think it will move in the near future, this book offers you ready-to-deploy market-specific strategies for bullish, bearish and sideways, i.e. range bound, market conditions.

New traders will especially benefit from this book as you will have a handy ready-reckoner to refer to in your journey of profitable options trading.

Alert:

Please note that lot sizes and trading rules mentioned in this book are as of January 2025. In keeping with evolving situations, National Stock Exchange of India changes rules and lot sizes from time to time. Please refer to https://www.nseindia.com/ for the latest information.

List of Abbreviations

ATM	At-the-Money.
ELM	Extreme Loss Margin.
ITM	In-the-Money.
IV	Implied Volatility.
LTP	Last Traded Price.
MTM	Mark-to-Market.
NSE	National Stock Exchange.
OI	Open Interest.
OTM	Out-of-the-Money.
PCR	Put-to-Call Ratio
SD	Standard Deviation.
SEBI	Securities and Exchange Board of India.
SPAN	Standard Portfolio Analysis of Risk.

Introduction

WELCOME TO THE FASCINATING WORLD of options trading. *Top 16 Options Trading Strategies — Simplified* is designed to be your guide and ready-reference for understanding and using the most powerful and profitable of options trading strategies, in sync with the prevailing market conditions. Whether you are just starting your options trading journey or you are an experienced trader looking to strengthen your trading odds, this book can help you profit from options trading.

Options trading offers a unique opportunity to leverage your capital and generate substantial returns, while at the same time managing risk effectively. Trading options can also, however, be an overwhelming experience for those unfamiliar with its intricacies. This book breaks down the seemingly complex world of options into an easy-to-understand and concise content from which every trader can benefit.

Once considered the domain of seasoned professionals, options trading has now become accessible to and popular among individual investors in India, thanks to advancements in technology and the increased availability of up-to-the-minute market information. By offering unique opportunities to profit from rising, falling and sideways markets, options have earned their rightful place as a crucial component of diversified investment portfolios worldwide.

This book will help you master 16 popular powerful and relatively easier to implement options trading strategies. These strategies are also eminently suitable for investors with limited capital seeking to profit from short-term market movements.

The book covers each of the 16 strategies in a concise manner. We will see:

- When to deploy each strategy;
- When to initiate the trade;
- How many legs, namely individual trades, are involved in the strategy;
- Each strategy's payoff, i.e. profit and loss scenarios, for different levels of market expiry;
- The breakeven points of every strategy, namely the point of no profit and no loss.

This will help you thoroughly grasp all important aspects of each strategy.

The book also explains what option Greeks Delta, Gamma, Vega and Theta are, and the important role each one plays in determining option premiums, and the impact the payoff from each strategy.

Whether you're looking for supplemental income, or striving to achieve financial independence through options trading, *Top 16 Options Trading Strategies — Simplified* is your gateway to a profitable journey in the fascinating world of options.

You must always keep in mind that successful options trading requires discipline, continuous learning, and the ability to adapt to ever-dynamic market scenarios.

So, come, let's embark on this thrilling voyage as we unravel the world of options trading, and empower you to become a confident and astute options trader, capable of navigating the complexities of financial markets with finesse and without fear.

Happy reading and prosperous trading ahead!

1

~

Basics of Options Trading

Concepts and Terminology

BEFORE PLUNGING INTO THE DETAILS of each of the 16 strategies, let's familiarize ourselves with some essential concepts and terminology that are used in the options trading game.

An option is a derivative contract that gives the buyer or the seller the right, without imposing any obligation, or compulsion, to buy or sell the underlying asset, called "underlying", by a certain date, known as the "expiration date", at the price specified in the contract, which is known as the "strike price", or simply the "strike."

A key thing to understand is that options trades can be, uniquely, non-directional trades. Non-directional trades, or market-neutral trades, are those trades where you can make money regardless of the direction of the underlying asset's price move, whether up, down, or sideways.

Call Options and Put Options

There are two types of options:

- Call options; and
- Put options.

Call options are bought when the trader expects the price of the underlying asset, whether it be a stock, an index, a currency, etc., to rise within a certain time frame.

On the other hand, **call options are sold** if the trader expects the price of the underlying asset to fall within a certain time frame.

Put options are bought when the trader expects the underlying's price to fall within a foreseeable time frame.

On the other hand, **put options are sold** if the trader expects underlying asset's price to rise within a time frame.

Options Terminology

Having a proper understanding of options terminology is very important. We will discuss and understand the various terms used in the options arena, including option chain, and open interest (OI), etc. using the January 2025 options series as the example. The date is not relevant since the concepts remain the same.

Option Chain

Go to https://www.nseindia.com/ in your browser and search for "NIFTY". Then go to the derivatives tab and there you will see the "Expiry Date" dropdown. Select any date, and you should see an options chain similar to the one shown in Table 1.1.

Let's now review the different sections of the option chain in Table 1.1.

Strike Price (Strike)

This is the price per unit of the underlying asset / share at which an option can be exercised, i.e. bought or sold. The strike price is listed in the middle column of the option chain, as you can see in Table 1.1.

Table 1.1

~

A Nifty Option Chain

					CALLS										PUTS					
OI	CHNG IN OI	Volume	IV	**LTP**	CHNG	BID Qty	BID Price	ASK Price	ASK Qty	**STRIKE Price**	BID Qty	BID Price	ASK Price	ASK Qty	CHNG	**LTP**	IV	Volume	CHNG IN OI	OI
33,946	-8,559	51,132	11.39	**729.00**	236.55	1,725	732.70	734.70	25	**23,700**	1,025	154.00	155.00	25	-139.45	**155.00**	15.04	93,503	-6,216	49,281
4,959	-801	5,095	11.16	**685.30**	221.90	250	681.95	701.85	25	**23,750**	25	164.50	167.90	25	-145.70	**167.90**	15.03	14,453	2,119	7,786
74,602	-12,695	95,376	11.71	**657.90**	223.30	600	653.90	660.00	125	**23,800**	25	179.15	183.00	25	-153.15	**180.90**	14.94	1,63,245	-3,145	96,102
3,768	129	6,905	11.42	**614.75**	211.10	250	612.65	621.00	75	**23,850**	25	194.00	210.40	500	-159.45	**195.80**	15.00	10,199	390	5,337
46,646	-8,090	69,488	11.72	**580.35**	200.85	50	581.65	589.95	25	**23,900**	50	208.05	209.80	25	-168.65	**208.05**	14.88	93,828	-643	65.261
3,770	1,015	9,314	11.50	**550.00**	196.05	25	550.00	562.50	25	**23,950**	250	219.05	229.00	25	-177.65	**224.20**	14.81	9,303	-117	4,177
1,55,545	-10,944	2,31,589	11.62	**515.50**	188.05	25	515.55	519.80	25	**24,000**	25	241.70	242.00	1,075	-186.45	**242.00**	14.81	2,51,356	18,499	2,25,687
2,312	300	9,141	11.55	**486.15**	181.35	500	475.85	491.85	25	**24,050**	900	250.60	260.00	250	-194.05	**258.50**	14.72	7,230	1,037	3,157
16,972	2,622	42,407	11.65	**458.75**	176.45	350	452.20	458.70	2,825	**24,100**	350	270.00	279.00	50	-199.95	**278.00**	14.67	41,473	5,373	17,651
3,636	564	8,281	11.72	**426.35**	165.20	50	421.75	429.40	25	**24,150**	50	291.00	298.45	25	-209.10	**298.00**	14.68	7,552	1,917	3,090
38,796	10,642	88,396	11.73	**399.90**	158.90	50	392.05	399.90	100	**24,200**	950	315.10	320.00	25	-215.65	**320.00**	14.69	87,962	31,104	61,962
3,795	1,219	9,883	11.77	**367.45**	147.50	100	360.40	376.00	50	**24,250**	50	338.00	343.25	200	-219.95	**343.30**	14.60	5,547	1,637	3,997
24,010	4,648	52,085	11.72	**346.15**	143.55	375	338.65	346.15	1,750	**24,300**	300	362.00	363.50	75	-325.60	**363.50**	14.59	22,523	7,120	18,278
3,055	622	5,033	11.63	**307.35**	124.25	500	305.55	315.85	25	**24,350**	250	379.15	388.85	1,225	-240.35	**386.80**	14.54	2,530	1,016	2,816
19,975	-521	37,289	11.61	**290.00**	121.60	75	287.80	292.00	50	**24,400**	50	408.00	414.85	25	-247.90	**414.80**	14.63	12,656	1,102	14,517
4,628	96	5,717	11.59	**268.70**	114.75	500	256.95	268.60	1,700	**24,450**	500	423.30	440.20	1,525	-251.55	**437.00**	14.46	767	82	1,162
97,960	3,906	1,77,683	11.50	**242.80**	103.30	25	240.75	245.00	75	**24,500**	25	461.30	464.55	175	-271.30	**465.75**	14.50	32,722	216	59,771
3,898	1,308	15,685	11.52	**221.60**	95.85	25	220.80	227.05	250	**24,550**	100	480.65	504.55	25	-268.35	**492.65**	14.44	269	32	856
20,786	1,308	51,034	11.40	**199.50**	85.90	2,000	197.05	199.50	3,375	**24,600**	525	507.80	525.45	25	-289.65	**516.10**	14.30	4,058	-126	5,881
4,803	991	7,361	11.36	**180.15**	78.00	250	174.60	186.15	250	**24,650**	300	530.30	565.90	100	-315.45	**549.55**	14.31	392	-	1,606
35,672	2,411	55,319	11.33	**162.95**	71.45	50	161.50	162.95	250	**24,700**	25	580.00	592.05	25	-299.95	**582.00**	14.34	2,077	427	8,340
5,307	770	22,368	11.26	**146.00**	63.75	25	146.00	155.60	250	**24,750**	75	605.40	638.95	200	-297.20	**622.80**	14.67	282	200	1,048
47,322	-141	90,080	11.22	**131.00**	57.85	25	130.05	131.10	25	**24,800**	25	648.00	656.80	100	-300.95	**653.05**	14.55	2,198	-27	6,508
3,902	1,563	9,897	11.23	**118.10**	52.70	250	112.20	119.75	75	**24,850**	100	670.65	699.75	325	-390.35	**683.75**	14.40	42	-22	380
36,605	-58	53,827	11.14	**104.05**	44.80	1,000	103.35	109.90	250	**24,900**	25	719.50	737.60	25	-319.35	**719.60**	14.43	993	-20	2,785
2,566	548	11,470	11.12	**92.85**	40.65	275	92.25	100.00	50	**24,950**	100	748.50	782.80	200	-405.85	**747.25**	14.05	50	-9	673
1,80,572	4,871	3,00,459	11.11	**83.00**	35.95	100	82.50	83.00	600	**25,000**	2,650	796.00	800.00	100	-336.30	**802.00**	14.86	13,645	-753	65,726

Call (CE)

As we noted, a call is an options contract that gives a trader the right to buy the underlying at the strike price (strike). You can see the various available call options on the left side of the strike price column in Table 1.1.

Put (PE)

Put is an options contract that gives a trader the right to sell the underlying at the strike price. You can see the various available puts on the right side of the strike price column in Table 1.1.

Last Traded Price (LTP)

This is the price, also known as premium, a trader pays for buying an option, or the price a trader receives upon selling an option.

At-the-Money Option (ATM)

An option is said to be at-the-money (ATM) if the market price of the underlying is equal to the option's strike price.

Thus, for example, if Nifty is trading at 19600, then the 19600 option strike will be an ATM option.

In-the-Money Option (ITM)

A call option is said to be in-the-money (ITM) when the underlying's price is higher than the option's strike price.

ITM Call Option: MP > SP

For example, if Nifty is trading at 19600, then the 19500 call will be an ITM option.

A put option, on the other hand, is said to be in-the-money (ITM) when the underlying's price is lower than the strike price.

ITM Put Option: MP < SP

For example, if Nifty is trading at 19600 then the 19700 put will be an ITM option.

Out-of-the-Money (OTM) Option

A call option is out-of-the-money (OTM) when the underlying's price is lower than the strike price. For example, if Nifty is trading at 19600, then the 19700 call will be an OTM strike.

A put option is said to be OTM when the underlying's price is higher than the strike price. For example, if Nifty is trading at 19600, then the 19500 put will be an OTM strike.

Open Interest (OI)

Open interest is the number of contracts bought or sold for a particular strike price. OI position can be found at the extreme right and left columns, respectively, of the option chain, as in Table 1.1.

How Open Interest Reveals the Market Sentiment

Open interest also reveals the prevailing market sentiment.

- If the underlying's price rise is accompanied by an increase in OI, the market sentiment is considered to be bullish. Basically, it demonstrates that traders are making fresh positions reflected by an increase in OI expecting the underlying's price to rise further from current levels.
- On the other hand, if the underlying price falls and OI also reduces, the sentiment is thought to be bearish. This would suggest that more and more traders are closing their positions, resulting in a fall in OI, expecting the underlying's price to go down further.
- There can also be a scenario where the price of an asset is rising while OI is falling. This may occur if there isn't any significant opening of new positions. This could be due to various factors, such as uncertainty, lack of interest from

traders, or market conditions that deter new positions. Open interest can also decline if certain derivative contracts are nearing their expiration date and traders are neither rolling them over nor opening new positions in the same contracts.

Thus, open interest can be influenced by factors beyond just the price movement, including trading behaviour, market sentiment, and contract expiration dynamics.

Change in OI

Adjacent to the open interest (OI) column, there is the column called, "Change in OI" which shows the number of contracts added or removed by traders during the day for that particular strike price.

Implied Volatility (IV)

Implied volatility is the market's forecast of the likely future movement of the underlying stock's or index's price. Higher implied volatility suggests that the underlying's price is likely to fluctuate more. This, in turn, results in its options commanding higher premium — and *vice versa*.

Trading Lot (Lot)

Trading lot is the number of underlying's shares that constitutes a single derivative trading unit. It is important to understand that in derivatives trading you can't trade a single share, or any arbitrary number of shares, of the underlying. You can only trade a designated lot, or multiple lots, of the underlying's shares.

Derivative Expiry

Every derivative has an expiry date. As the name suggests, expiry is the date when the concerned option contract expires; namely it is the date after which the right to buy or sell conferred by the option stands extinguished.

In India, the Nifty expiry date is of three types:

- **Current month expiry**, which is the last Thursday of the ongoing month.
- **Near-month expiry**, which is the last Thursday of the next month.
- **Far-month expiry**, which is the last Thursday of the month after the next one.

Say, we are in the month of July XXXX, then July XXXX Nifty contract will be the current month, August XXXX Nifty contract will be the near month, and September XXXX Nifty contract will be the far month. Expiry would happen on the last Thursday of each of the three respective months for Nifty. Similarly, for BankNifty, expiry would happen on the last Wednesday of each of the three respective months.

In 2019, NSE introduced weekly expiring options for indexes. As the name suggests, these are option contracts which expire on a weekly basis. Also, the trading cycle of weekly options is entirely independent of the monthly expiries discussed above. Till November 2024, we had weekly expiries for many indexes but after November 2024, we have weekly expiry for Nifty only, along with its monthly expiry. Rest all indexes have now only monthly expiries.

Please note that for individual stocks, however, only monthly expiring options are available.

In this book, we will only be discussing option strategies with monthly expiry contracts.

Breakeven Point

This is the underlying's price point above which you will start to lose money in the case of a PE — or start earning money in the case of a CE.

For example, let's assume that you have purchased a call option of Nifty 19600 strike at an option premium of ₹50. When you buy a call option, you will stand to earn money if Nifty moves up quickly. As the buyer, your breakeven price will be at Nifty 19650, namely the strike price, *plus* the option premium you paid. If Nifty moves above 19650, then you will profit as a CE buyer. If, however, the underlying's price moves below 19650, you will start losing money.

On the other hand, if you are a seller of the Nifty 19600 strike call option at a premium of ₹50, you will earn money so long as Nifty stays below the 19650 level, namely below the strike price *plus* the option premium received. In this case, the breakeven point will be Nifty at 19650. If the market moves above 19650, the option seller will start to lose money.

Similarly, suppose you have purchased a put option of Nifty 19600 strike at an option premium of ₹50. When you buy a put option, you will stand to earn money if Nifty moves down quickly. As the buyer, your breakeven price will be 19550, namely the strike price, minus the option premium you paid. If Nifty moves below 19550, then you will be in profit as the PE buyer. If, however, the underlying Nifty level goes above 19550, you will start losing money.

On the other hand, if you are a seller of the Nifty 19600 strike put option at a premium of ₹50, then you will earn money so long as Nifty stays above the 19550 level, namely the strike price *minus* the option premium received. In this case the breakeven point will be 19550. If the market moves below 19550, the option seller will start to lose money.

Table 1.2

Breakeven of Call Options and Put Options

Call Options			
	Breakeven Point	*Profit Level*	*Loss Level*
CE Buyer	Strike + Premium	Underlying price above breakeven	Underlying price below breakeven
CE Seller	Strike + Premium	Underlying price below breakeven	Underlying price above breakeven
Put Options			
PE Buyer	Strike – Premium	Underlying price below breakeven	Underlying price above breakeven
PE Seller	Strike – Premium	Underlying price above breakeven	Underlying price below breakeven

Risk Reward Ratio

Before initiating any trade, you should work out its risk-reward ratio. This is the ratio of how much capital you are willing to risk for a certain reward. Let's suppose that you expect to collect a premium of ₹10,000 in a particular options trade. Now, if the maximum risk, i.e. the maximum possible loss, in the trade is ₹15,000, then the risk-reward ratio will be 1.5:1.

In case you sell options using a hedged multi-leg strategy, something which we will discuss and explore in later chapters, then the extent of risk is well defined. On the other hand, if you trade using naked options you must place a stop loss to protect yourself from unacceptable losses. Since the stop loss has only a one-day validity, you have to place a stop loss afresh every trading morning. If you are an option buyer, then the maximum risk will be limited to the premium paid for buying that option. Theoretically reward can be unlimited for option buyers.

Options Premium or Options Price

Option premium is the amount an option buyer pays to buy an option and, correspondingly, the amount an option seller receives on selling the option.

The option premium is made up of two components, namely:

- Intrinsic value, and
- Extrinsic value.

Intrinsic value reflects the actual value existing in the option were it to expire today. It arises from an interplay between the option's strike price and the underlying's current market price.

Extrinsic value, also known as time value, is determined by the time remaining till the option's expiration, the implied volatility (IV) of the underlying asset, dividends, and interest rates. **Extrinsic value is that portion of an option's premium which is in excess of its intrinsic value before expiration.** Other factors being the same, the longer the time period before expiry, higher would be the option's time value. At the time of expiry, the time value becomes zero.

Time value = Option premium – Intrinsic value

So to arrive at an option's time value, whether for a call option or a put option, you first need to determine its intrinsic value, and then subtract that intrinsic value from the option premium. Whatever remains will be the option's time value.

A few key points to remember about option premium:

- Intrinsic value is the value of exercising an in-the-money (ITM) option.
- At-the-money (ATM) options and out-of-the-money (OTM) options have no intrinsic value; they have only extrinsic value.
- At expiration an option will only have intrinsic value, if any.

Options Greeks at a Glance

Option prices are sensitive to, namely impacted, by:

- Changes in the underlying's price;
- Changes in the expected volatility; and
- The passage of time.

Collectively, these factors which lead to changes in an option's premium are called "the Greeks" and offer the trader a conceptual framework to judge the exposure of one's trades to various factors that affect an option's price.

Following are the four main Greeks:

- Delta;
- Gamma;
- Vega; and
- Theta.

Delta

Delta is the most important of the option Greeks. Delta measures how an option's premium, i.e. the option's price, changes with respect to any change in the underlying's price.

The value of Delta ranges from −1 to 1.

In general, call options have a positive Delta, the value of which ranges from 0 to 1. This means that calls have a positive relationship with Delta and therefore the price of the underlying and the call option's price move in the same direction.

Put options, on the other hand, in general have a negative Delta, the value of which ranges from −1 to 0. This means that puts have a negative relationship with Delta. The negative Delta value of a put option indicates that the option's price and the underlying's price move in opposite directions to each other.

Finally, the closer Delta's value is to 1, the greater will be the move in the option's price when the underlying's price moves by ₹1.

Concept of Neutral Delta

As highlighted above, call options have a positive delta and put options have a negative delta. Accordingly:

- Being long on a call, i.e. buying a call, will result in a positive Delta. Conversely, being short on a call, i.e. selling a call, results in a negative Delta.
- Being long on a put, i.e. buying a put, results in negative Delta. Conversely, being short on a put, i.e. selling a put, results in positive Delta.

Another feature of Delta is that it indicates the option's probability of being ITM at expiration. Suppose a particular option strike has a Delta of 0.20. Now, 0.20 Delta tells us that there are 20% chances of that option becoming ITM at the time of expiry. If an option has a Delta of 0.30, it suggests that there is a 30% chance of the option finishing in-the-money at expiry. So, basically, the absolute value of Delta gives us the approximate probability of that option finishing in-the-money at expiry.

Please keep in mind that traders usually refer to the Delta in absolute form. For example, a 0.25 Delta is usually referred to as a 25 Delta, and so on.

Let's say we sell 5 call options of 0.4 Delta, i.e. 40 Delta each. We then have a Delta position of 40 x 5 = −200.

In order to be Delta neutral, we must either:

- Sell put options having cumulative Delta of +200; or
- Buy call options of the next expiry, having a cumulative Delta of +200.

By doing so, our position then becomes zero Delta, or Delta neutral. We can use this concept to deploy delta neutral trading setups, which will be discussed later in the book.

Delta Neutral Trading

Delta neutral trading uses strategies that simultaneously deploy multiple trades (legs) having both positive and negative Delta in a manner that the overall trade position does not react to small changes in the underlying's price. Consequently, whether the underlying's price goes up or down, the trade maintains its value. We will use this Delta neutral concept to construct neutral and hedged strategies for options trading, described later in the book.

Gamma

Gamma conveys the rate at which Delta would change with a changes in the underlying's price. Like Delta, Gamma too is dynamic. **Gamma starts increasing when the underlying's price starts approaching the option's strike price.**

ATM strikes have the highest Gamma. That's because the ATM strike's Delta is most sensitive to the underlying's price movement.

On the other hand, Gamma falls in the case of ITM or OTM strikes.

Vega

Vega is related to implied volatility (IV) and shows how much the option premium would change for each percentage change in the underlying's implied volatility. **As a rule, higher the underlying's volatility, the more expensive its option's contract is.** Option sellers will benefit in high volatility conditions because they will collect higher option premiums which will translate into more money being collected per lot. On the other hand, when volatility is low options too will trade at lower premiums. If an options trader buys an option at this point, and if the volatility subsequently goes up, premiums will also go up and option buyers will be benefited.

Vega is always the highest for ATM strikes, and reduces if we go to ITM or OTM strikes.

The value of Vega also depends on the time remaining for the option's expiry. Thus, for the same strike price, Vega of the next month's expiry will always be more than that for the current month's expiry.

Theta

Theta measures the fall in an option's premium due to the passage of time (time decay). Simply stated, it tells us how much the premium will reduce with each passing day till the option's expiry. For this reason, **Theta is always negative for all long options and positive for all short options.**

In the upcoming chapters we will see how option Greeks impact option premiums in various strategies.

Summary

In this chapter we have discussed some important concepts that you need to clearly grasp in order to trade options profitably. These will also help you in better understanding the trading strategies that follow. I would suggest that you may wish to re-read this chapter, if necessary, until you fully grasp these concepts.

2

~

Our Top 16 Options Trading Strategies

AS SET OUT IN THE INTRODUCTION, this book explores 16 popular and effective option trading strategies. When trading options, you can then easily pick a suitable strategy for different market conditions, bullish, bearish, or neutral (sideways). We will also discuss strategies which can help you hedge, namely protect, your investments. We will be covering the following options strategies in this book.

Bullish Strategies

- Bull call spread;
- Bull put spread;
- Call ratio back spread; and
- Bear call ladder.

Bearish Strategies

- Bear call spread;
- Bear put spread;
- Put ratio back spread; and
- Bull put ladder.

Neutral Strategies

- Long straddle;
- Short straddle;
- Long strangle;
- Short strangle;
- Iron butterfly; and
- Iron condor.

Hedging Strategies

- Synthetic call options; and
- Synthetic put options.

We will start our journey with strategies which help you profit when you have a bullish view of the market. I request new traders to go through these bullish strategies repeatedly till you fully grasp all their nuances.

Once you fully understand the logic and application of these bullish strategies, it would be easier for you to understand bearish, neutral and hedging strategies as well. So please consider bullish strategies as the building block in your journey of learning options trading, and try to master them thoroughly.

Payoff tables are also provided for each strategy. Payoff table in options trading refers to a tabular representation of potential profits or losses that an option trader can expect based on different outcome scenarios. It typically includes columns representing different prices of the underlying asset at expiration, and rows representing different option strategies or positions. The table shows the resulting payoff, i.e. profit or loss, for each combination of the underlying's price and option position. Such a tabular presentation helps traders analyse and make decisions based on potential outcomes under different market conditions. Looking at the sample payoff table for different strategies, new traders should try to plot the payoff table in Microsoft Excel for different spot and strike prices in order to clarify their concepts.

Part 1

~

Bullish Strategies

— for When You Expect the Price Will Rise

3

~

Bull Call Spread

THIS IS THE FIRST OF THE BULLISH STRATEGIES which we will discuss.

First, we will consider the key features of bull call spread in a concise manner. We will then review this strategy's payoff diagram and payoff table to enable you to understand the profit and loss scenarios for different levels of market expiry. Finally, we will review the effect of option Greeks on a bull call spread.

Bull Call Spread in a Nutshell

Bull call spread is a 2-leg strategy which you should deploy:

- When you are moderately bullish on the market.
- Accordingly, you want to profit when the market moves up;
- But at the same time you want to limit your losses if the market were to sharply decline instead. And, for that, you accept a lower cap on profits.
- Both the maximum loss and maximum profit are capped and pre-defined.
- Initial net debit strategy.

Table 3.1 encapsulates the bull call spread in a nutshell, to give you a quick fix on how it works.

Table 3.1

Bull Call Spread in a Nutshell

	When to Use a Bull Call Spread When you have a moderately bullish view about the market / underlying and believe that it may move up a little bit from its current levels.
	Trade Setup Bull call spread is 2-leg strategy, generally comprising simultaneously: — Leg 1: Buying one ATM Call (CE); and — Leg 2: Selling one (equal quantity) OTM Call of higher strike (CE). Both legs have the same expiration date and the same underlying.
	Breakeven Point The point of no profits and no losses for this strategy is: Lower strike (ATM CE strike) + Net Debit.
	Profit Scenarios You will make a profit if the underlying expires above the breakeven point. The maximum profit is capped at: Spread *minus* Net Debit.
	Loss Scenarios You will make a loss if the underlying expires below the breakeven point. The maximum loss is capped at the net debit of the trade.
	Risk Reward Ratio ▪ Maximum risk (₹50) is below the breakeven point considering trade has been initiated as per levels mentioned in Table 3.2, and ▪ Maximum reward (₹50) is above the breakeven point considering that trade has been initiated as per levels mentioned in Table 3.2 So, risk reward ratio here is 1:1.

(Contd . . .)

Table 3.1: **Bull Call Spread in a Nutshell** *(. . . contd.)*

	Volatility Impact Strategy benefits by an increase in volatility.
	When to Initiate the Trade Ideally you should enter the trade 25 trading days — i.e. about three-and-a half-weeks — ahead of expiry. You will get a good premium by starting early.
	When to Exit the Trade You should exit the trade: ▪ As soon as the pre-defined maximum profit (₹50) is reached (at 15,500 in the trade) if the trade has been initiated as per levels mentioned in Table 3.2, or ▪ The stop loss is hit, or ▪ One week before expiry, whichever event occurs first.

Payoff Diagram

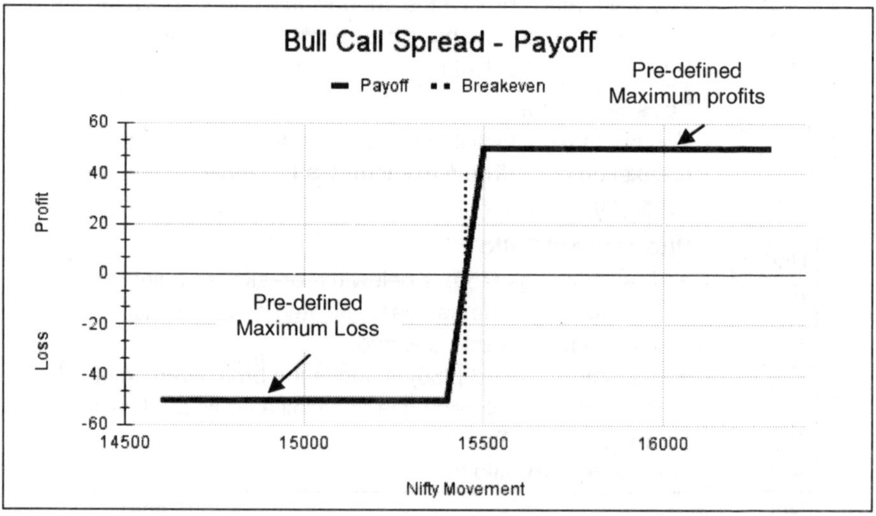

Figure 3.1: **Payoff Diagram for a Bull Call Spread**

Figure 3.1 is the payoff diagram for a bull call spread. As depicted by the graph, profits and losses are both capped and well-defined for this strategy.

Hypothetical Nifty Bull Call Spread

Table 3.2 summarizes the particulars of our hypothetical Nifty trade. We are considering the example of a Nifty trade since Nifty is the most widely traded derivative in India.

As indicated by Table 3.2, we initiate our hypothetical bull call spread trade with Nifty at 15425 spot levels. Bull call spread being a 2-leg strategy:

- For the first leg we buy one at-the-money call option (ATM 15400CE) for ₹122. That will be our debit (out of pocket) as we are buying an option.
- For the second leg we will sell one, namely an equal quantity higher strike, out-of-the-money call option (OTM 15500CE) of the same expiry for ₹72. This will be our credit — money coming in — as we are selling an option.

Table 3.2

Our Hypothetical Nifty Bull Call Spread

Particular	*Value*
Underlying	Nifty
Spot Price (₹)	15425
Buy ATM CE	15400
Sell OTM CE	15500
Debit from buying ATM call (₹)	–122
Credit from selling OTM call (₹)	72
Net (Debit) (₹)	–122 + 72 = –50

- Our net debit here will be ₹50 (72 − 122 = − ₹50).
- Since OTM options will always be cheaper than ATM options, and as we are buying an ATM option and selling an OTM option, there will always be an initial net debit in a bull call spread.

Payoff Table

When the underlying Nifty moves in either direction, there will be a certain profit or loss. Table 3.3 illustrates the payoff, i.e. profit / loss, scenarios for various levels of Nifty expiry. For ease of understanding there is a 100-point difference between each hypothetical Nifty expiry.

For this trade the breakeven point will be the lower ATM CE strike + net debit. Which means the breakeven point will be at Nifty 15400 + 50 = 15450.

- Accordingly, if Nifty expires below 15450, you will make a defined or fixed loss, capped at the net debit.
- On the other hand, if Nifty expires above 15450 you will make a defined, i.e. fixed profit, capped at Spread *minus* Net Debit.
- If Nifty expires at 15450 you will neither make a profit nor a loss, as this is our trade's breakeven point.

Table 3.3

Payoff Table for Different Levels of Nifty Expiry

Market Expiry	*Long ATM CE Strike 15400 Intrinsic Value (₹)*	*Long ATM CE Strike 15400 Payoff (₹)*	*Short OTM CE Strike 15500 Intrinsic Value (₹)*	*Short OTM CE Strike 15500 Payoff (₹)*	*Strategy Payoff (₹)*	*Comments*
14,600	0	−122	0	72	−50	Limited Loss Zone. Loss capped at Net Debit.
14,700	0	−122	0	72	−50	
14,800	0	−122	0	72	−50	
14,900	0	−122	0	72	−50	
15,000	0	−122	0	72	−50	
15,100	0	−122	0	72	−50	
15,200	0	−122	0	72	−50	
15,300	0	−122	0	72	−50	
15,400	0	−122	0	72	−50	
15,450	50	−72	0	72	0	Breakeven Point.
15,500	100	−22	0	72	50	Limited Profit Zone. Profit Capped at Spread Minus Net Debit.
15,600	200	78	100	−28	50	
15,700	300	178	200	−128	50	
15,800	400	278	300	−228	50	
15,900	500	378	400	−328	50	
16,000	600	478	500	−428	50	
16,100	700	578	600	−528	50	

How Greeks Impact the Payoff

Having grasped the payoff table for different Nifty expiries (Table 3.3), let's now understand the relationship between the underlying's price movement and the various option Greeks for a bull call spread. We will not get into calculating the Greeks, but will focus instead on trying to understand how the various Greeks impact the payoff from this strategy.

Payoff *vis-à-vis* Delta

The long call option in a bull call spread, ATM 15400CE in our trade, has a positive Delta. This means that if the price of the underlying rises, the value of the long call option will also increase. The Delta will typically be close to +0.5 for an at-the-money (ATM) call option, and will rise as the option moves further in the money (ITM). As you would recall, Delta represents the percentage of movement in the option's price relative to the underlying asset's price movement.

The short call option in a bull call spread, OTM 15500CE in our hypothetical trade, has a negative Delta. This means that as the price of the underlying asset rises, the value of the short call option will fall. The Delta of the short call option will be close to −0.5 for an ATM call option, and will reduce as the option moves further ITM.

The combination of an ATM long call option having a higher positive Delta, and an OTM short call option with a lower negative Delta, creates a net positive Delta for the bull call spread strategy. This means that the overall trade benefits from a rise in the underlying's price, as the gains from the long call option will outweigh the losses from the short call option. You can see this demonstrated in Table 3.3.

However, the Delta of a bull call spread is not as high as that of a standalone (naked) long call option. The short call option limits the potential upside of the strategy, and as the stock price moves above the short call's strike price, the gains from this strategy will get capped at a pre-defined level.

However the bull call spread limits your loss at a lower level were the market to declines.

Payoff *vis-à-vis* Gamma

The long call option, ATM 15400CE in our hypothetical bull call spread trade, has a positive Gamma. As the price of the underlying asset rises, the Gamma of the long call option causes its Delta to increase. This means that the long call option becomes more sensitive to changes in the underlying asset's price, resulting in greater potential gains as the underlying asset's price rises. On the other hand, it also means that losses would accelerate if the underlying's price declines.

The short call option leg in a bull call spread, OTM 15500CE in this case, has a negative Gamma. As the price of the underlying asset rises, the Gamma of the short call option causes its Delta to fall. This means that the short call option becomes less sensitive to changes in the underlying asset's price, which limits the possible losses from the short call option if the underlying asset's price were to rise. Conversely, it also means that gains from the short call option will be limited if the underlying asset's price declines.

The combination of an ATM long call option with a higher positive Gamma, and a short call option having lower negative Gamma in a bull call spread leads to an overall positive Gamma for this strategy. This implies that as the underlying asset's price rises, Delta of the overall position will increase, leading to a magnified potential for profits with favourable price movements.

Payoff *vis-à-vis* Vega

The ATM long call option in a bull call spread has higher a positive them Vega. Any increase in implied volatility will therefore generally increase the value of the long call option. Remember, higher implied volatility, in turn, leads to higher option prices, resulting in potential profits for the long call option. Conversely, if implied volatility were to fall, the price of the long call option may fall, potentially leading to losses.

On the other hand, the OTM short call option in a bull call spread has a negative Vega. This means that any increase in implied volatility will generally reduce the value of the short call option. Lower implied volatility then leads to lower option prices, resulting in potential profits for the short call option.

The bull call spread strategy combines the ATM long call option's higher positive Vega and the OTM short call option's lower negative Vega. The overall position will thus have a positive Vega bias. This means that an increase in implied volatility will generally benefit the overall strategy, potentially leading to higher profits. On the other hand, a fall in implied volatility may adversely affect the overall strategy's gains.

Payoff *vis-à-vis* Theta

At the initiation of a bull call spread, the overall effect of Theta is generally negative owing to the long ATM CE. The strategy involves buying and selling call options, resulting in both long and short positions. The ATM long call option typically has a higher premium due to its closer proximity to the prevalent market price of the underlying asset. As time passes, the premium of the ATM long call option will reduce due to time decay (negative Theta), resulting in a fall in the strategy's overall value.

The effect of Theta becomes more pronounced as time passes, and the options approach expiration. While both the long and the short call option will experience time decay, the ATM long call option will lose value at a faster rate due to its higher premium and closer proximity to the underlying asset's price. If the underlying asset's price remains relatively stable, or experiences only a small move, the bull call spread's value will fall over time due to the negative effect of Theta.

As the options approach expiration, the rate of time decay accelerates leading to steeper declines in option values. If the underlying asset's price is trading between the strike prices of the two call options involved in the spread, the overall impact of Theta can be more pronounced, potentially leading to significant losses.

If the underlying asset's price moves significantly in the desired direction, namely upward for a bull call spread, the impact of Theta can be mitigated, or even reversed. As the strategy becomes profitable, gains from the long call option can outweigh losses from the short call option.

Summary

In this chapter we have studied:

- Complete set-up and working of the bull call spread strategy.
- The resultant payoffs from it at different expiry levels.
- How Greeks impact the payoff from this strategy.

Let's now move on to our second bullish strategy.

4

~

Bull Put Spread

THIS IS THE SECOND BULLISH STRATEGY we will explore.

First we will consider the bull put spread strategy in a concise manner. Thereafter we will review this strategy's payoff diagram and payoff table to enable you to visualize the various profit and loss scenarios for different expiry levels. Finally we will review the effect of option Greeks on a bull put spread.

Bull Put Spread in a Nutshell

Bull put spread is a 2-leg strategy which you should employ:

- When you have a moderately bullish view of the market.
- Accordingly, the goal is to be able to make some profits when the market moves up.
- While at the same time you want to limit your losses if the market were to decline sharply.
- Both the maximum loss and maximum profit are capped and pre-defined.
- Initial net credit strategy.

Table 4.1 encapsulates bull put spread in a nutshell for you to get a quick fix on how this strategy works.

Table 4.1

Bull Put Spread in a Nutshell

Bull Put Spread in a Nutshell
When to Use a Bull Put Spread When you have a moderately bullish view on the market and believe that the market is likely to move up a little bit from its current levels.
Trade Setup Bull put spread is a 2-leg net credit strategy comprising simultaneously: — Leg 1: Buying one OTM Put (PE) of a higher strike; — Leg 2: Selling one (equal quantity) ITM Put (PE). Both legs have the same expiration and the same underlying.
Breakeven Point The breakeven point for this strategy is: ITM PE strike *minus* net credit.
Profit Scenarios You will make profit if the underlying expires above the breakeven point. The maximum profit would be capped at the premium different between the two strikes.
Loss Scenarios You will make a loss if the underlying expires below the breakeven point. Maximum loss = Spread – Net Credit
Risk Reward Ratio ▪ Maximum risk (₹110) is below the breakeven point if the trade has been initiated as per levels mentioned in Table 4.2. ▪ Maximum reward (₹90) is above breakeven point considering trade has been initiated as per levels mentioned in Table 4.2. So, risk reward ratio here is 11:9.
Volatility Impact Strategy benefits by reduced volatility.

(Contd . . .)

Table 4.1: **Bull Put Spread in a Nutshell** *(. . . contd.)*

	When to Initiate the Trade Ideally you should enter the trade 25 days — about three-and-a-half weeks — ahead of expiry. You will get a good premium by starting early.
	When to Exit the Trade You should exit the trade: ▪ As soon as the pre-defined maximum profit (₹90) is reached (at 15,600 in the trade) if the trade has been initiated as per levels mentioned in Table 4.2, or ▪ The stop loss is hit, or ▪ One week before expiry, whichever event occurs first.

Payoff Diagram

Figure 4.1 is the payoff diagram for a bull put spread. As depicted by the graph, profits and losses are both clearly pre-defined for this strategy.

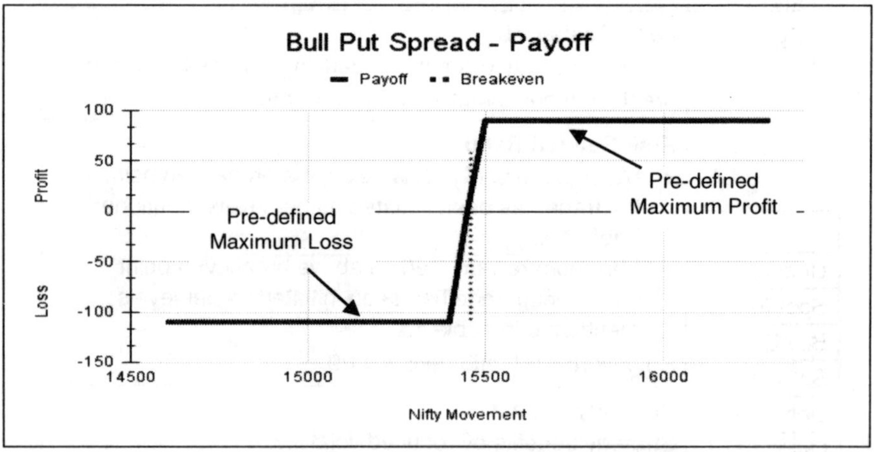

Figure 4.1: **Payoff Diagram for a Bull Put Spread**

Hypothetical Nifty Bull Put Spread

The payoff graph of a bull put spread is quite like that of the bull call spread, but the underlying option legs and fundamentals are completely different as we will now see below.

Table 4.2 displays the particulars of our hypothetical Nifty trade. We will consider the strategy with the example of a hypothetical Nifty trade since Nifty is the most widely traded derivative in India.

Let's say we initiate a bull put spread trade with Nifty at 15425 spot levels. To deploy this two-legged strategy:

- As the first leg we buy one out-of-the-money put option (OTM 15350PE) for ₹85. That will be our debit as we are buying an option.
- For the second leg we will sell one (equal quantity) higher strike in-the-money put option (ITM 15550PE) for ₹175. That will be our credit as we are selling an option.
- Our net credit here will be ₹90 (175 − 85 = 90).
- Since OTM options will always be cheaper than ITM options, and we are selling an ITM option and buying an OTM option, there will always be an initial net credit in this strategy.

Table 4.2

Our Hypothetical Nifty Bull Put Spread

Particular	*Value*
Underlying	Nifty
Spot Price	15425
Buy OTM PE	15350
Sell ITM PE	15550
Debit from buying 1 OTM PUT	− 85
Credit from selling 1 ITM PUT	175
Net Credit (₹)	−85 + 175= 90

Payoff Table

When the underlying Nifty moves in either direction, there will be a certain profit or loss. Table 4.3 illustrates the payoff, i.e.

Table 4.3

Payoff Table for Different Levels of Nifty Expiry

Market Expiry	*Long OTM PE Strike 15350 Intrinsic Value (₹)*	*Long OTM PE Strike 15350 Payoff (₹)*	*Short ITM PE Strike 15550 Intrinsic Value (₹)*	*Short ITM PE Strike 15550 Payoff (₹)*	*Strategy Payoff (₹)*	*Comments*
14,600	750	665	950	−775	−110	Loss Zone. Maximum Loss Capped at Spread Minus Net Credit.
14,700	650	565	850	−675	−110	
14,800	550	465	750	−575	−110	
14,900	450	365	650	−475	−110	
15,000	350	265	550	−375	−110	
15,100	250	165	450	−275	−110	
15,200	150	65	350	−175	−110	
15,300	50	−35	250	−75	−110	
15,400	0	−85	150	25	−60	
15,460	0	-85	90	85	0	Breakeven Point.
15,500	0	−85	50	125	40	Profit Zone. Profit Capped at Net Credit.
15,600	0	−85	0	175	90	
15,700	0	−85	0	175	90	
15,800	0	−85	0	175	90	
15,900	0	−85	0	175	90	
16,000	0	−85	0	175	90	
16,100	0	−85	0	175	90	

profit / loss, scenarios for various levels of Nifty expiry. For ease of understanding there is a 100-point difference between each hypothetical Nifty expiry.

The breakeven point for this strategy will be the ITM PE strike *minus* net credit. In our example this will translate to ₹15,550 – ₹90 = ₹15,460. Thus:

- If Nifty expires below 15460, you will make a defined, i.e. fixed, loss.
- If Nifty expires above 15460, you will make pre-defined, i.e. fixed, profits.
- If Nifty expires at 15460 you will neither make a profit nor lose any money as this is our breakeven point.

Bull Put Spread *versus* Bull Call Spread

The bull put spread is similar to a bull call spread in terms of profit and loss scenarios — but with one fundamental difference. A bull put spread is invoked for net credit. However, as we saw in the previous chapter, a bull call spread is invoked for net debit.

A bull call spread involves call options and it benefits from a rise in the underlying asset's price. A bull put spread, on the other hand, involves put options and profits from price stability, or a moderate rise in the underlying asset's price. Both strategies have limited risk and limited potential profit.

Traders need to consider their market outlook before choosing between a bull put spread and the bull call spread. A bull call spread is deployed when the underlying asset's price is expected to rise from its current level. On the other hand, a bull put spread is deployed when the underlying asset's price is expected to stay above a certain level (above higher strike sold — ITM PE).

A bull call spread benefits from increased volatility, while the bull put spread benefits from lower volatility.

A bull put spread generally has a lower upfront cost than the bull call spread.

It's essential to analyse your expectations for the underlying asset's price movement before choosing between the bull call spread and the bull put spread.

How Greeks Impact the Payoff

Having grasped the payoff scenarios for different Nifty expiries from Table 4.3, let's now understand the relationship between the underlying's price movement and the various option Greeks for a bull put spread. We will not get into calculating the Greeks, but will focus instead on trying to understand how the various Greeks impact the payoff from this strategy.

Payoff *vis-à-vis* Delta

The short ITM put option leg in a bull put spread, 15550PE in this case, has a positive Delta. This means that if the price of the underlying asset rises, the value (price) of the short put option will fall, resulting in profit from this leg. The Delta of the short put option will typically be close to +0.5 for an at-the-money (ATM) put option and will increase as the option moves further in-the-money (ITM).

On the other hand, the long OTM put option leg in a bull put spread, 15350PE in this case, has a negative Delta. This means that as the price of the underlying asset rises, the value of the long put option will fall, resulting in a loss from this leg. The

Delta of the long put option will be close to −0.5 for an ATM put option, and will reduce as the option moves further ITM.

The combination in a bull put spread of a short ITM put option with a positive Delta, and a long OTM put option having a negative Delta, creates an overall positive Delta for the strategy. This means that the trade benefits from a rising underlying, as the gains from the short put option will outweigh the losses from the long put option.

Payoff *vis-à-vis* Gamma

The short ITM put option in a bull put spread has a negative Gamma. As the price of the underlying asset moves away from the strike price, whether up or down, the Gamma of the short put option causes its Delta to become more sensitive to further price changes. This can be beneficial for the strategy, as it reduces potential losses from the short put option leg if the price of the underlying asset rises.

The long OTM put option in a bull put spread has a positive Gamma. As the price of the underlying moves away from the strike price, whether upward or downward, the Gamma of the long put leg causes its Delta to become more sensitive to further price changes. This can be a risk for the strategy, as it can lead to potential losses from the long put option were the underlying asset's price to rise significantly.

In a bull put spread, the combination of an ITM short put option with a positive Gamma, and a long OTM put option having a negative Gamma, creates an overall positive Gamma for this strategy. This implies that, overall, this trade benefits from larger price movements in the underlying asset. As the underlying asset's price rises, the Delta of the overall position increases, potentially resulting in larger profits.

Payoff *vis-à-vis* Vega

The short ITM put option leg in a bull put spread has a negative Vega. This means that any increase in implied volatility will generally lead to an increase in the value of the short put option leg. A higher implied volatility leads to higher option prices, which can result in potential losses for this leg. Conversely, if the implied volatility reduces, the value of the short put option may fall, potentially leading to gains.

The long OTM put option leg in a bull put spread has a positive Vega. This means that any increase in implied volatility will raise the value of this leg. Lower implied volatility, in turn, leads to lower option prices, which can result in potential losses for the long put option leg. Conversely, if implied volatility increases, the value of the long put option will rise, potentially leading to gains.

The bull put spread strategy combines a short ITM put option leg, having negative Vega, and an OTM long put option leg, which has a positive Vega, resulting in a net overall negative Vega for the trade position. This means that any decrease in implied volatility will, overall, generally benefit the strategy, potentially leading to higher profits. On the other hand, any rise in implied volatility may adversely affect the strategy's overall value.

Payoff *vis-à-vis* Theta

At the initiation of a bull put spread, the overall effect of Theta is generally positive. This is because the strategy involves both selling and buying put options, resulting in both short and long positions. The ITM short put option leg typically has a higher premium due to its closer proximity to the prevalent market price of the underlying. As time passes, the value of the ITM short put option will reduce due to time decay (positive Theta), resulting in potential profits for the strategy.

As the options approach expiration, the effect of Theta becomes more pronounced. Both the short and long put options will experience time decay, but the ITM short put option with a higher premium will lose value at a faster rate due to its closer proximity to the underlying price. If the underlying asset's price remains relatively stable, or experiences only small moves, the bull put spread's overall value will increase over time due to the positive effect of Theta.

Approaching expiration, the rate of time decay of the options accelerates, leading to steeper declines in option prices. If the underlying asset's price is trading above the ITM short put option's strike price, the impact of Theta can be more pronounced, potentially leading to significant profits.

If the underlying asset's price moves significantly in the desired direction, namely upward for a bull put spread, the impact of Theta can get mitigated, or even reversed. As the strategy becomes profitable, the gains from the short put option can outweigh the losses from the long put option.

Summary

In this chapter we have discussed:

- Complete set-up and working of the bull put spread strategy.
- How the bull put spread strategy works;
- The payoffs at different expiry levels.
- How the Greeks impact the payoff from this strategy.

Let's now move on to our next bullish strategy.

5

~

Call Ratio Back Spread

THIS IS THE THIRD in our group of bullish strategies.

First we will review this strategy in a concise manner. We will then look at a payoff diagram as well as a payoff table to enable you to visualize various profit and loss scenarios for a range of market expiries. Finally, we will review the impact of option Greeks in the case of a call ratio back spread.

Call Ratio Back Spread in a Nutshell

The call ratio back spread is a multi-leg credit strategy which you can advantageously deploy when:

- You have a bullish view of the market.
- Volatility is high. Volatility can be measured from the IV item listed in the Option Chain explained in Chapter 1: "Basics of Options Trading", or by looking at India VIX, explained in a later part of the book.

Together, the above two factors mean that you expect the market to rise sharply from its current levels.

The key characteristic of the call ratio back spread is its potential for high, theoretically unlimited, profits when the underlying moves significantly higher.

- With a bullish view and a volatile market, you would naturally want to make big profits in case the market moves up.
- But at the same time you would want to limit your losses should the market decline sharply instead.
- Typically structured as net credit strategy.
- The gains from the rising underlying are sight to be made by move calls.

Table 5.1

Call Ratio Back Spread in a Nutshell

	When to Use Call Ratio Back Spread ▪ When you are bullish on the market and think that the price will move up quickly from its current levels. ▪ And when volatility is high.
	Trade Setup Call Ratio Back Spread is a multiple-leg credit strategy comprising buying net selling calls (CE): — Leg-1: Selling one ITM Call (CE); — Legs-2 and 3: Buying two OTM Call (CE).
	Breakeven Points There will be two points of no profits and no losses, namely two breakeven points, in this strategy: ▪ One, in case the underlying's price moves lower, and ▪ The second in case the underlying moves up (*see* Table 5.3).
	Profit Scenarios ▪ You will make bigger, potentially unlimited, profits if the underlying expires above the higher breakeven point. ▪ If the underlying expires below the lower breakeven point, you will still make nominal profits (*see* Table 5.3).

(Contd . . .)

Table 5.1: **Call Ratio Back Spread in a Nutshell** *(. . . contd.)*

	Loss Scenarios You will make a pre-defined maximum loss if the underlying expires in between the lower and the higher breakeven points.
	Risk Reward Ratio ▪ Maximum risk (₹150) is at 15500 level in the case of our hypothetical trade (*see* Table 5.2). ▪ Maximum reward is unlimited once the upper breakeven point is breached. ▪ Limited reward (₹50) below the lower breakeven point in our hypothetical trade (*see* Table 5.2).
	Volatility Impact Strategy gets benefitted by increased volatility.
	When to Initiate the Trade Ideally you should enter the trade 25 days — about three-and-a-half weeks — ahead of expiry. You will get a good premium by starting early.
	When to Exit the Trade You should exit the trade: ▪ When price becomes stagnant and volatility starts falling, or ▪ The stop loss is hit, or ▪ One week before expiry, whichever event occurs first.

Payoff Diagram

Figure 5.1 is the payoff diagram for a call ratio back spread. As depicted by the graph, while profits are potentially unlimited as the price rises, but losses, including the maximum loss, are pre-defined.

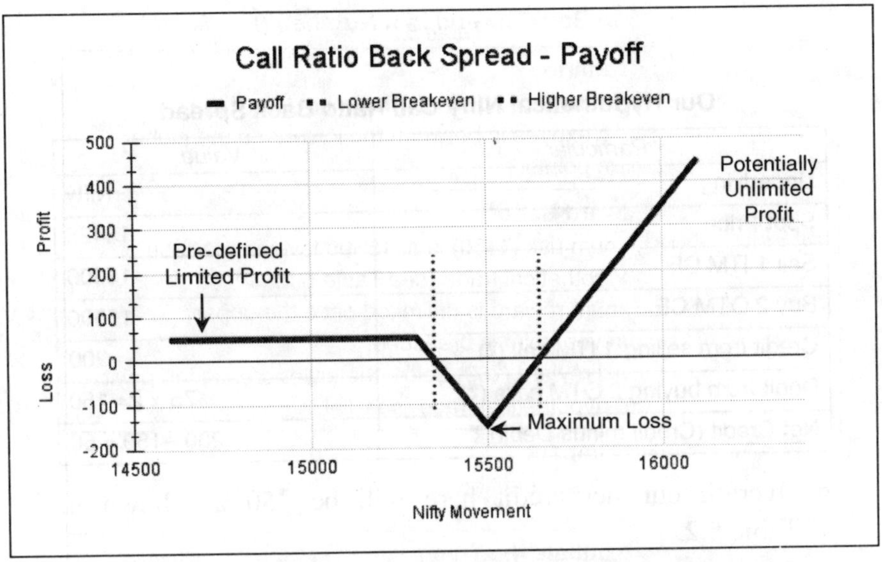

Figure 5.1: **Payoff Diagram for a Call Ratio Back Spread**

Hypothetical Call Ratio Back Spread

Let us now consider this strategy by way of an example. Table 5.2 summarizes the particulars of our hypothetical Nifty trade. We are considering the example of a Nifty trade since Nifty is the most widely traded derivative in India.

Let us assume that hypothetical call ratio back spread trade is initiated with Nifty at 15,425 spot levels. To deploy our 3-leg trade:

- For the first leg we will sell one in-the-money call option (ITM 15300CE) for ₹200. That will be our credit as we are selling an option.
- For the second and third legs we will buy two out-of-the-money call options of a higher strike (OTM 15500CE) for ₹75 each. That will be our debit as we are buying options.

Table 5.2

Our Hypothetical Nifty Call Ratio Back Spread

Particular	*Value*
Underlying	Nifty
Spot Price	15425
Sell 1 ITM CE	15300
Buy 2 OTM CE	15500
Credit from selling 1 ITM call (₹)	200
Debit from buying 2 OTM calls (₹)	75 × 2= 150
Net Credit (Credit minus Debit) ₹	200 –150 = 50

- Overall, our net credit here will be ₹50 as shown in Table 5.2.

Since OTM options will always be cheaper than ITM options, and you are selling one ITM call option and buying two OTM call options, there will always be an initial net credit in this strategy.

Payoff Table

As the underlying Nifty moves in either direction, there will be a certain profit or loss. Table 5.3 illustrates the payoff, i.e. profit / loss, scenarios for various levels of Nifty expiry. For ease of understanding we have considered a 100-point difference between each hypothetical Nifty expiry.

From Table 5.3 you can see that:

- The lower and higher breakeven points are 15350 and 15650, respectively.
- If Nifty expires above 15650, you will make increasingly bigger profits at higher Nifty expiries. Even if Nifty expires below 15350, you will still make pre-determined nominal profits as shown in Table 5.3.

Table 5.3

Payoff Table for Different Levels of Nifty Expiry

Market Expiry	*Short ITM CE Strike 15300 Intrinsic Value (₹)*	*Short ITM CE Strike 15300 Payoff (₹)*	*Long OTM CE Strike 15500 Intrinsic Value (₹)*	*Long OTM CE Strike 15500 Payoff (₹)*	*Strategy Payoff (₹)*	*Comments*
14,600	0	200	0	−150	50	Limited Profit Zone.
14,700	0	200	0	−150	50	
14,800	0	200	0	−150	50	
14,900	0	200	0	−150	50	
15,000	0	200	0	−150	50	
15,100	0	200	0	−150	50	
15,200	0	200	0	−150	50	
15,300	0	200	0	−150	50	
15,350	50	150	0	−150	0	Lower Breakeven Point.
15,400	100	100	0	−150	−50	Loss Zone. Max Loss Capped.
15,500 (Max Loss)	200	0	0	−150	−150	
15,600	300	−100	100	50	−50	
15,650	350	−150	150	150	0	Upper Breakeven Point.
15,700	400	−200	200	250	50	Rising Profit Zone. Potentially Unlimited Profit.
15,800	500	−300	300	450	150	
15,900	600	−400	400	650	250	
16,000	700	−500	500	850	350	
16,100	800	−600	600	1,050	450	

- If Nifty expires at exactly 15350, or at exactly 15650, you will neither make a profit nor a loss as these are our two breakeven points.
- If Nifty expires anywhere between 15350 and 15650, you will incur losses as shown in payoff table and payoff diagram. The maximum loss occurs if the Nifty expires at 15500.

How Greeks Impact the Payoff

Let's now understand the relationship between the underlying's price movement and various option Greeks in the case of a call ratio back spread. We will not be calculating the Greeks, but will focus instead on trying to understand how the various Greeks impact the payoff from this strategy.

Payoff *vis-à-vis* Delta

Each of the two OTM long call options in a call ratio back spread has a positive Delta value. This means that the value of the long call options will increase as the price of the underlying rises. The Delta of ATM long call options is typically close to +0.5, and reduces as the options move further OTM.

The ITM short call option leg in a call ratio back spread has a negative Delta value. This means the value of the short call option will fall as the price of the underlying asset rises. The Delta of the short call option is typically close to −0.5 for ATM options, and falls as the option moves further OTM.

The combination of two long call options with a positive Delta and a short call option having negative Delta in a call ratio back spread creates an overall positive Delta for the strategy. This means that our trade will benefit from a rise in the underlying's price, since the resultant gains in the option's price from the long call options will outweigh the losses from the short call option.

Payoff *vis-à-vis* Gamma

Each of the two OTM long call options in a call ratio back spread has a positive Gamma value. As the price of the underlying rises, the positive Gamma of these two long call options boosts their Delta to become even more positive, potentially moving closer to +1. This means that the values of the long call options become more sensitive to increases in the underlying asset's price, amplifying the potential gains as the underlying asset's price rises, in according our market view .

The ITM short call option in a call ratio back spread has a negative Gamma value. As the price of the underlying asset rises, the Gamma of the short call option causes its Delta to become even more negative, potentially moving closer towards −1. This means that the value of the short call option becomes more sensitive to any further increases in the underlying's price. This can be a risk for the strategy, as it may lead to potential losses from the short call option leg if the underlying asset's price rises significantly.

The combination of two long call options having a positive Gamma, and a short call option with negative Gamma in a call ratio back spread, creates an overall positive Gamma for the strategy. This implies that the overall trade benefits from larger price movements in the underlying asset. As the underlying's price rises, the Delta of the overall position is further boosted by the positive Gamma, resulting in potentially larger profits.

Payoff *vis-à-vis* Vega

Each of the two long OTM call options in a call ratio back spread has a positive Vega. An increase in implied volatility will therefore generally increase the price of the long call options, resulting in gains in the values of these long call options. Remember, the existence of high volatility is the key reason for selecting this strategy. Conversely, if the implied volatility reduces, the price of the long call options may fall, potentially leading to losses.

The ITM short call option in a call ratio back spread has a negative Vega. This means that any increase in implied volatility will generally increase the value of the short call option, which will lead to higher option prices, potentially leading to losses from the short call leg of this strategy.

The call ratio back spread strategy combines two long call options, each having a positive Vega, and a short call option with negative Vega, resulting in an overall positive Vega for the strategy. Any increase in implied volatility will therefore generally benefit this strategy, potentially leading to higher profits. On the other hand, a fall in implied volatility may adversely affect the strategy's overall value.

The positive Vega from the two long call options amplifies the potential gains when the implied volatility rises, allowing the trade to benefit from higher option prices.

Payoff *vis-à-vis* Theta

At the initiation of the call ratio back spread, the overall effect of Theta is generally negative. This is because the strategy involves buying and selling call options, resulting in both long and short positions. Long call options have negative Theta meaning they lose value over time due to time decay. Short call option has positive Theta, meaning it gains value as time passes because seller benefits from the decay in the option's prices. If the underlying asset's price remains relatively stable, or experiences only small moves, the call ratio back spread's value will decrease over time due to the negative effect of Theta.

As the options approach expiration, the rate of time decay accelerates leading, in turn, to steeper declines in option values. If the underlying asset's price is trading above the strike prices of the long call options, the impact of Theta can be more pronounced, potentially leading to significant profits.

Summary

In this chapter we have discussed:

- Complete working and set-up of a call ratio back spread is.
- The resultant payoffs from the strategy at different market expiry levels.
- How Greeks impact the payoff from this strategy.

Let's now go on to our next bullish strategy.

6

~

Bear Call Ladder

THIS IS THE FOURTH AND FINAL STRATEGY in our group of bullish strategies.

First we will review the bear call ladder in a concise manner. Thereafter we will consider the strategy's payoff diagram and payoff table to enable you to visualize the various profit and loss scenarios for different levels of market expiry. Finally we will review the effect of option Greeks on a bear call ladder.

Bear Call Ladder in a Nutshell

Bear call ladder is the strategy to employ:

- When volatility is high;
- You have a bullish view of the market; and
- You expect the underlying to move up quickly.

With a bear call ladder you will stand to make big profits if the underlying moves up. At the same it would limit your losses in case the underlying were to decline sharply, instead of going up.

Bear call ladder is an enhancement of the call ratio back spread strategy and should be used only when you are very confident that the market will move up from its current levels.

Table 6.1 encapsulates the bear call spread in a nutshell, for you to get a quick fix on how this strategy works.

Table 6.1

Bear Call Ladder in a Nutshell

	When to use a Bear Call Ladder If you are very bullish on the market and think that the market will move up quickly from its current levels.
	Trade Setup Bear call ladder is a three-leg strategy, comprising: — Leg-1: Selling one ITM Call (CE); — Leg-2: Buying one ATM Call (CE); — Leg-3: Buying one OTM Call (CE).
	Breakeven Point There are two breakeven points in this strategy — one in case the underlying moves lower and a second one if the underlying moves up instead.
	Profit Scenarios You will make bigger profits if the underlying expires above the higher breakeven point. If the underlying expires below the lower breakeven point, you will, however, still make nominal profits.
	Loss Scenarios You will make a loss if the underlying expires between the lower and higher breakeven points.
	Risk Reward Ratio ▪ Maximum risk (₹150) is between breakeven points considering trade has been initiated as per levels mentioned in Table 6.2, and ▪ Maximum reward is unlimited once upper breakeven point is breached ▪ Limited reward (₹50) is below lower breakeven point considering trade has been initiated as per levels mentioned in Table 6.2

(Contd . . .)

Table 6.1: **Bear Call Ladder in a Nutshell** *(. . . contd.)*

	Volatility Impact Strategy gets benefitted by increased volatility.
	When to Initiate the Trade Ideally you should enter the trade 25 days — about three-and-a-half weeks — ahead of expiry. You will get a good premium by starting early.
	When to Exit the Trade You should exit the trade: ▪ When price becomes stagnant and volatility starts falling, or ▪ The stop loss is hit, or ▪ One week before expiry, whichever event occurs first.

Payoff Diagram

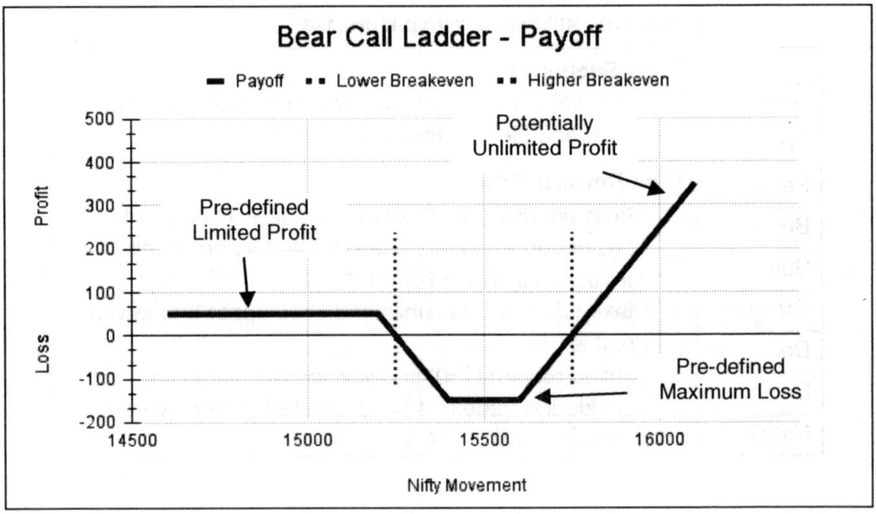

Figure 6.1: **Payoff Diagram for a Bear Call Ladder**

Figure 6.1 is the payoff diagram for a bear call ladder. As depicted by the graph, profits could be unlimited, but the maximum loss is pre-defined for this strategy.

Table 6.2 shows the particulars of our hypothetical Nifty trade. We are considering a Nifty trade since Nifty is the most widely traded derivative in India.

We initiate our hypothetical trade with Nifty at 15425 spot levels. Bear call ladder is a three-legged strategy. To deploy this strategy:

- As the first leg we will sell one in-the-money call option (ITM 15200CE) for ₹300. That will be our credit as we are selling an option.
- For the second leg we will buy one at-the-money call option (ATM 15400CE) for ₹175. That will be a debit leg as we are buying an option.

Table 6.2

Our Hypothetical Nifty Bear Call Ladder

Particular	*Value*
Underlying	Nifty
Spot Price	15425
Sell 1 ITM CE	15200
Buy 1 ATM CE	15400
Buy 1 OTM CE	15600
Credit from ITM Sale (₹)	300
Debit from ATM Buy (₹)	175
Debit from OTM Buy (₹)	75
Net Credit (₹)	300 – 175 –75 = 50

- For the third leg we will buy one out-of-the-money call option (OTM 15600CE) for ₹75. That will also be a debit leg as we are buying an option.
- Our net credit here will thus be ₹50 (300 − 175 − 75) = ₹50).
- Since ATM and OTM options will always be cheaper than ITM options, and you are selling ITM options and buying ATM and OTM options, there will always be an initial net credit in a bear call ladder.

Payoff Table

When the underlying Nifty moves in either direction, there will be a certain profit or loss. Table 6.3 illustrates the payoff, i.e. profit / loss, scenarios for various levels of Nifty expiry. For ease of understanding there is a 100-point difference between each hypothetical Nifty expiry.

From Table 6.3, you can see that:

- The lower and higher breakeven points are 15250 and 15750, respectively.
- If Nifty expires above 15750, you will make good profits.
- Even if Nifty expires below 15250, you will still make nominal profits as shown in Table 6.3.
- If Nifty expires either at exactly 15250 or exactly at 15750 you will not make a profit nor lose money as these are our two breakeven points.
- If Nifty expires between 15250 and 15750, you will incur losses as shown in the payoff table and graph.

Table 6.3

Payoff Table for Different Levels of Nifty Expiry

Market Expiry	*Short ITM Strike 15200 Intrinsic Value (₹)*	*Short ITM Strike 15200 Payoff (₹)*	*Long ATM Strike 15400 Intrinsic Value (₹)*	*Long ATM Strike 15400 Payoff (₹)*	*Long OTM Strike 15600 Intrinsic Value (₹)*	*Long OTM Strike 15600 Payoff (₹)*	*Strategy Payoff (₹)*	*Comments*
14,600	0	300	0	−175	0	−75	50	Limited Profit Zone.
14,700	0	300	0	−175	0	−75	50	
14,800	0	300	0	−175	0	−75	50	
14,900	0	300	0	−175	0	−75	50	
15,000	0	300	0	−175	0	−75	50	
15,100	0	300	0	−175	0	−75	50	
15,200	0	300	0	−175	0	−75	50	
15,250	50	250	0	−175	0	−75	0	Lower Breakeven Point.
15,300	100	200	0	−175	0	−75	−50	Limited Loss Zone.
15,350	150	150	0	−175	0	−75	−100	
15,400	200	100	0	−175	0	−75	−150	
15,500	300	0	100	−75	0	−75	−150	
15,600	400	−100	200	25	0	−75	−150	
15,650	450	−150	250	75	50	−25	−100	
15,700	500	−200	300	125	100	25	−50	
15,750	550	−250	350	175	150	75	0	Higher Breakeven Point.
15,800	600	−300	400	225	200	125	50	Rising Profit Zone. Potentially Unlimited Profit.
15,900	700	−400	500	325	300	225	150	
16,000	800	−500	600	425	400	325	250	
16,100	900	−600	700	525	500	425	350	

How Greeks Impact the Payoff

Let's now understand the relationship between the underlying's price movement and various option Greeks for a bear call ladder. We will not get into calculating the Greeks, but will focus instead on trying to understand how the various Greeks impact the payoff from this strategy.

Payoff *vis-à-vis* Delta

The 15,400 ATM long call option in a bear call ladder will have a positive Delta value. Accordingly, as the price of the underlying asset rises, so will the value of the long call option. The Delta of the long call option is typically close to +0.5 for ATM options, and reduces as the option moves further OTM.

The 15,600 OTM long call option also has a positive Delta value, though not as much as that of the ATM call. This means that as the price of the underlying rises, the value (price) of the OTM long call option will also increase.

The ITM short call option (15200CE in this case) in a bear call ladder will have a negative Delta value. This means that if the price of the underlying rises, the value of the short call option will fall. The Delta of the short call option will typically be close to −0.5 for ATM options and will increase as the option moves further OTM.

The combination of long call options with positive Delta and a short call option having a negative Delta creates an overall positive Delta for the bear call ladder. This means that the overall position benefits from a rise in the underlying's price, as gains from the long call options will outweigh losses from the short call option.

The key characteristic of a bear call ladder is its potential for unlimited profits if the underlying asset experiences a significant upside move. The positive Delta from the long call options then amplifies the potential gains as the underlying's price rises, allowing the strategy to effectively participate in this upward price movement.

Payoff *vis-à-vis* Gamma

The ATM long call option in a bear call ladder has a positive Gamma value. As the price of the underlying asset rises, Gamma of the long call options causes their Delta to become more positive, potentially moving closer to +1. This means that long call options become more responsive to further increases in the underlying asset's price, enhancing the potential gains if the underlying's price rises.

The OTM long call option in a bear call ladder also has a positive Gamma value. As the price of the underlying asset rises, the Gamma of the long call option causes its Delta to become more positive, potentially moving closer to +1. This means that the long call option becomes more responsive to further increases in the underlying asset's price. This can be beneficial for the strategy, as it enhances potential gains if the underlying's price rises.

The ITM short call option in a bear call ladder has a negative Gamma value. As the price of the underlying asset rises, the Gamma of the short call option causes the Delta to become more negative, potentially moving closer to −1. In other words, this short call option becomes more responsive to further increases in the underlying's price. This can be a risk for the strategy, as it may lead to potential losses from the short call option leg if the underlying asset's price rises significantly.

The combination of long call options, with a positive Gamma, and a short call option having negative Gamma in a bear call ladder creates an overall positive Gamma for the strategy. This implies that the strategy benefits from larger price movements in the underlying asset. As the underlying's price rises, the Delta of the overall position increases, potentially resulting in larger profits.

The key characteristic of the bear call ladder is its potential for unlimited profits if the underlying asset experiences a significant up move. That's because the positive Gamma from the long call options amplifies the potential gains as the asset's price rises, allowing the strategy to effectively participate in the asset's upward price movement.

Payoff *vis-à-vis* Vega

The ATM long call option in a bear call ladder has a positive Vega. This means that any increase in implied volatility will generally increase the value of this long call option. A higher implied volatility leads to higher option prices, which can result in potential gains for the long call option. Conversely, if the implied volatility reduces, the value of the long call option may also fall, potentially leading to losses.

The OTM long call option in a bear call ladder has a positive Vega. This means that any increase in implied volatility will generally increase the value of this long call option. Higher implied volatility leads to higher option prices, which can result in potential gains from this long call option leg. Conversely, if the implied volatility reduces, the value of the long call option may fall, potentially leading to losses.

The ITM short call option — 15200CE in this case — in a bear call ladder has a negative Vega. This means that any rise in implied volatility will generally increase the value of the short call option, which will adversely impact this strategy's profitability. A lower implied volatility leads to lower option prices, which can result in potential gains for the short call option.

The bear call ladder strategy combines long call options, which have positive Vega, and a short call option with negative Vega, resulting in an overall positive Vega for the strategy. This means that any increase in implied volatility will generally benefit the strategy, potentially leading to bigger profits. On the other hand, a fall in implied volatility may adversely affect the overall strategy's value.

The key characteristic of the bear call ladder is its potential for unlimited profits if the underlying asset makes a significant up move. The positive Vega from the long call option legs amplifies the potential gains as implied volatility increases, allowing the strategy to benefit from higher option prices.

Payoff *vis-à-vis* Theta

At the initiation of the bear call ladder, the overall effect of Theta is generally negative. This is because the strategy involves buying and selling call options, resulting in both long and short positions. Long call options have negative Theta meaning they lose value over time due to time decay. Short call option has positive Theta, meaning it gains value as time passes because seller benefits from the decay in the option's prices. If the underlying asset's price remains relatively stable, or experiences only small moves, the bear call ladder's value will decrease over time due to the negative effect of Theta.

As the options approach expiration, the rate of time decay accelerates leading, in turn, to steeper declines in option values. If the underlying asset's price is trading above the strike prices of the OTM long call options, the impact of Theta can be more pronounced, potentially leading to significant profits.

Summary

In this chapter we have discussed:

- How the bear call ladder strategy works;
- What will be the payoff from this strategy at different levels of the underlying's expiry;
- How Greeks impact the payoff of this strategy.

~

With this we conclude our discussion of bullish option trading strategies. In the book's next section, we will consider some great strategies for a bearish market.

Part 2

~

Bearish Strategies

— for When You Expect the Price Will Fall

7

~

Bear Call Spread

THIS IS THE FIRST OF THE BEARISH STRATEGIES covered in this book.

First we will see the bear call spread in a concise manner. Thereafter, we will see the strategy payoff diagram and a payoff table to enable you to visualize the various profit and loss scenarios for different levels of market expiry. Finally, we will review the impact of option Greeks on a bear call spread.

Bear Call Spread in a Nutshell

The bear call spread is a strategy which can be deployed when you are moderately bearish on the market. The strategy will enable you to make some profits when the market moves down, while at the same time limit your losses if the market goes up sharply.

Table 7.1 encapsulates the bear call spread in a nutshell to enable you to get an overview of its working.

Table 7.1

Bear Call Spread in a Nutshell

	When to Use Bear Call Spread When you are moderately bearish about the market and think that the market may move down a bit from its current levels. Also, this strategy will limit your losses if the market rises sharply instead.
	Trade Setup This is a two-leg strategy encompassing: — Leg-1: Buying one OTM Call (CE); and — Leg-2: Selling one ITM Call (CE).
	Breakeven Point The point of no profits and no losses for this strategy is: ITM strike + net strategy credit.
	Profit Scenarios You will make a pre-defined profit if the underlying expires below the breakeven point.
	Loss Scenarios You will make a pre-determined loss if the underlying expires above the breakeven point.
	Risk Reward Ratio ▪ Maximum risk (₹200) is above the breakeven point in our hypothetical trade (*see* Table 7.2), and ▪ Maximum reward (₹100) is below the breakeven point for our hypothetical trade (*see* Table 7.2). So, risk reward ratio here will be 2:1 in this case.
	Volatility Impact Strategy gets benefitted by decreased volatility.
	When to Initiate a Bear Call Spread Ideally you should initiate the trade 25 days, i.e. about 3-and-a-half weeks, ahead of expiry. You will get a good premium by starting early.

(Contd . . .)

Table 7.1: **Bear Call Spread in a Nutshell** *(. . . contd.)*

	When to Exit the Trade You should exit the trade: ▪ As soon as the pre-defined maximum profit is reached. For our hypothetical trade (*see* Table 7.2) the maximum profit is ₹100 at 15,300 levels ▪ The stop loss is hit, or ▪ One week before expiry, whichever event occurs first.

Payoff Diagram

Figure 7.1 is the payoff diagram for a bear call spread. As depicted by the graph, both maximum profits and losses are predefined for this strategy.

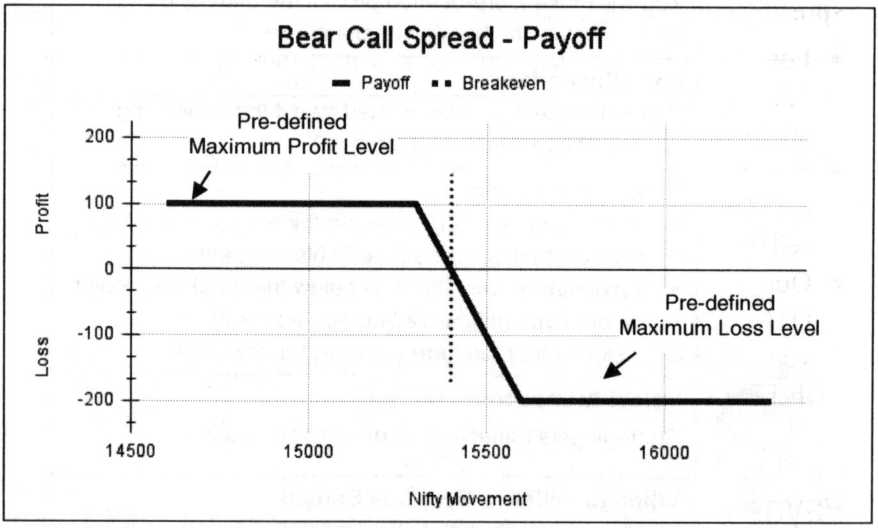

Figure 7.1: **Payoff Diagram for a Bear Call Spread**

Table 7.2

Our Hypothetical Nifty Bear Call Spread

Particular	*Value*
Underlying	Nifty
Spot Price	15425
Buy OTM CE	15600
Sell ITM CE	15300
Debit from long call (₹)	–50
Credit from short call (₹)	150
Net Credit (₹)	–50 + 150 =100

Table 7.2 details the particulars of our hypothetical Nifty bear call spread trade. Let's say we initiate a bear call spread in Nifty at 15425 spot levels. We deploy the two-legged bear call spread strategy as follows:

- For the first leg we buy one out-of-the-money (OTM 15600CE) call option for ₹50. That will be our debit as we are buying an option.
- For the second leg we sell one in-the-money call option (ITM 15300CE) for ₹150. That will be our credit as we are selling an option.
- Our net credit here will be ₹100 (150 – 50 = 100). Since OTM options will always be cheaper than ITM options, and you are buying an OTM option and selling an ITM option, there will always be a net initial credit in this strategy.

Payoff Table

When the underlying Nifty moves in either direction, there will be a certain profit or loss. Table 7.3 illustrates the payoff, i.e.

profit / loss, scenarios for various levels of Nifty expiry. For ease of understanding there is a 100-point difference between each hypothetical Nifty expiry.

Table 7.3

Payoff Table for Different Levels of Nifty Expiry

Market Expiry	*Long OTM CE Strike 15600 Intrinsic Value (₹)*	*Long OTM CE Strike 15600 Payoff (₹)*	*Short ITM CE Strike 15300 Intrinsic Value (₹)*	*Short ITM CE Strike 15300 Payoff (₹)*	*Strategy Payoff (₹)*	*Comments*
14,600	0	−50	0	150	100	Profit Zone. Profit Capped at Net Credit.
14,700	0	−50	0	150	100	
14,800	0	−50	0	150	100	
14,900	0	−50	0	150	100	
15,000	0	−50	0	150	100	
15,100	0	−50	0	150	100	
15,200	0	−50	0	150	100	
15,300	0	−50	0	150	100	
15,400	0	−50	100	50	0	Breakeven Point.
15,500	0	−50	200	−50	−100	Loss Zone. Maximum Loss Capped.
15,600	0	−50	300	−150	−200	
15,700	100	50	400	−250	−200	
15,800	200	150	500	−350	−200	
15,900	300	250	600	−450	−200	
16,000	400	350	700	−550	−200	
16,100	500	450	800	−650	−200	

The breakeven point for this strategy will be:

ITM strike + net credit.

This will translate into the Nifty level of 15300 + 100 = 15400.

- If Nifty expires below 15400, you will make a pre-defined profit.
- Conversely, if Nifty expires above 15400, you will make a defined fixed loss.
- If Nifty expires at 15400, you will neither profit nor lose as this is the breakeven point.

How Greeks Impact the Payoff

Let's understand the relationship between the underlying's price movement and the various option Greeks for a bear call spread. We will not get into calculating the Greeks, but will focus instead on trying to understand how the various Greeks impact the payoff for this strategy.

Payoff *vis-à-vis* Delta

The short call option in a bear call spread has a negative Delta. This means that as the price of the underlying asset falls, the value of the short call option (15300CE in this case) will increase, which will benefit the trade. The Delta of the short call option will typically be close to −0.5 for ATM options, and will increase as the option moves further OTM.

The long call option in a bear call spread has a positive Delta. This means that as the price of the underlying asset falls, the value of the long call option (15600CE in this case) will reduce. The

Delta of the long call option will typically be close to +0.5 for ATM options, and will reduce as the option moves further OTM.

The combination of a short call option, having a negative Delta, and a long call option with positive Delta creates an overall negative Delta for a bear call spread. Accordingly, the overall trade position benefits from a fall in the underlying asset's price. **The strategy aims to profit from a small fall in the underlying asset's price, but is not designed to profit from significant declines.** The Delta of a bear call spread is not as low as that of a standalone short call option. The long call option limits the potential of the strategy, and as the stock price moves below the breakeven point, the strategy's gains will be capped.

Payoff *vis-à-vis* Gamma

The short call option in a bear call spread has a negative Gamma value. As the price of the underlying asset falls, the Gamma of the short call option (15300CE in this case) causes its Delta to become more negative, potentially moving closer to −1. This means that the short call option becomes more sensitive to any further falls in the underlying's price. This can be beneficial for the trade, as it enhances potential gains if the underlying asset declines.

The long call option in a bear call spread has positive Gamma values. As the price of the underlying asset falls, the Gamma of the long call option (15600CE in this case) causes its Delta to become more positive, potentially moving closer to 1. This implies that the long call option leg becomes more sensitive to further falls in the underlying asset's price. This impact is relatively weaker compared to that of the short call option's Gamma due to the higher strike price.

The combination of a short call option having negative Gamma and a long call option with positive Gamma in a bear call spread creates an overall mixed Gamma for the strategy.

This means that the trade benefits from bigger price movements in the underlying. As the underlying asset's price falls, the Gamma of the overall position increases, potentially resulting in larger profits.

Payoff *vis-à-vis* Vega

In a bear call spread the short call option has a negative Vega. This means that any increase in implied volatility will generally reduce the value of the short call option, 15300CE in this case. Lower implied volatility leads to lower option prices, which can result in potential gains from the short call option leg. Conversely, if implied volatility reduces, the value of the short call option may increase, potentially leading to losses.

The long call option — 15600CE in this case — in a bear call spread has a positive Vega. This means that an increase in implied volatility will generally increase the value of the long call option. Conversely, if implied volatility reduces, the value of the long call option leg may fall, potentially leading to losses.

The combination of a short call option having a negative Vega, and a long call option with positive Vega creates an overall negative Vega in a bear call spread. This means that any reduction in implied volatility will generally benefit the overall strategy. On the other hand, any increase in implied volatility may adversely affect the overall strategy's value.

Payoff *vis-à-vis* Theta

The short call option in a bear call spread, 15300CE in this case, has a positive Theta. Thus, as time passes, and all else being equal, the value of the short call option will fall. The Theta of the short call option will typically be higher for options with shorter time to expiration. This time decay is beneficial for the short call since it contributes to potential profits.

The long call option in a bear call spread, 15600CE in this case, has a negative Theta. All else being equal, as time passes the value of the long call option will also fall. The negative Theta of the long call option implies that the time decay works against the long call's potential profitability.

The combination of a short call option with positive Theta and a long call option having negative Theta creates a positive overall Theta in a bear call spread. Thus, as time passes the strategy generally benefits from time decay. The short call option contributes more to the positive Theta than the long call option's contribution to the negative Theta, resulting in a net positive Theta for the strategy.

Theta has a direct impact on the bear call spread strategy's profitability over time. As time progresses, the strategy's value increases due to the positive Theta. However, the limited profit potential and potential losses need to be considered. **Traders should aim to either close, or adjust, their position before expiration to capture the available profits, because the strategy's profitability may diminish nearer expiration.**

Summary

In this chapter we have discussed:

- How the bear call spread strategy works;
- What the payoff from it would be for different levels of underlying expiry.
- How the Greeks impact the payoff from this strategy.

8
~
Bear Put Spread

LET'S NOW GET TO GRIPS with our second bearish strategy.

First we will see review in bear put spread in a concise manner. Thereafter we will consider this strategy's payoff diagram and payoff table for you to understand the various profit and loss scenarios for different levels of market expiry. Finally, we will review the effect of option Greeks on a bear put spread.

Bear Put Spread in a Nutshell

Bear put spread is the strategy which you can deploy when:

- You are moderately bearish about the market.
- You want to make some profits when the market goes down.
- At the same time you want to limit your losses should the market move up sharply contrary to your expectation.

Table 8.1 encapsulates the bear put spread in a nutshell for you to get a quick overview on how it works.

Table 8.1

Bear Put Spread in a Nutshell

Bear Put Spread in a Nutshell
When to Use a Bear Put Spread If you are moderately bearish on the market and think that it could move down a little bit from its current levels.
Trade Setup A bear put spread is a two-leg strategy comprising: — Leg-1: Buying one ITM Put (PE); and — Leg-2: Selling one OTM Put (PE).
Breakeven Point The point of no profits and no losses for this strategy is: ITM strike *minus* net debit of the strategy.
Profit Scenarios You will make profits if the underlying expires below the breakeven point.
Loss Scenarios You will make a loss if the underlying expires above the breakeven point.
Risk Reward Ratio ▪ Maximum risk is above the breakeven point, and ▪ Maximum reward is below the breakeven point. For example, the risk reward ratio for our hypothetical trade will be 1:2 (*see* Table 8.2).
Volatility Impact Strategy gets benefitted by increased volatility.
When to Initiate a Bear Put Spread Ideally, you should enter the trade 25 days, i.e. about 3-and-a-half weeks, before expiry. You will get a good premium if you start early.

(Contd . . .)

Table 8.1: **Bear Put Spread in a Nutshell** *(. . . contd.)*

	When to Exit the Trade You should exit the trade: ▪ As soon as the pre-defined maximum profit is reached. In our hypothetical trade that level is 15,300 (*see* Table 8.2), or ▪ When the stop loss is hit, or ▪ One week before expiry, whichever event occurs first.

Payoff Diagram

Figure 8.1 is the payoff diagram for a bear put spread. As depicted by the payoff graph, profits and losses are both capped for this strategy.

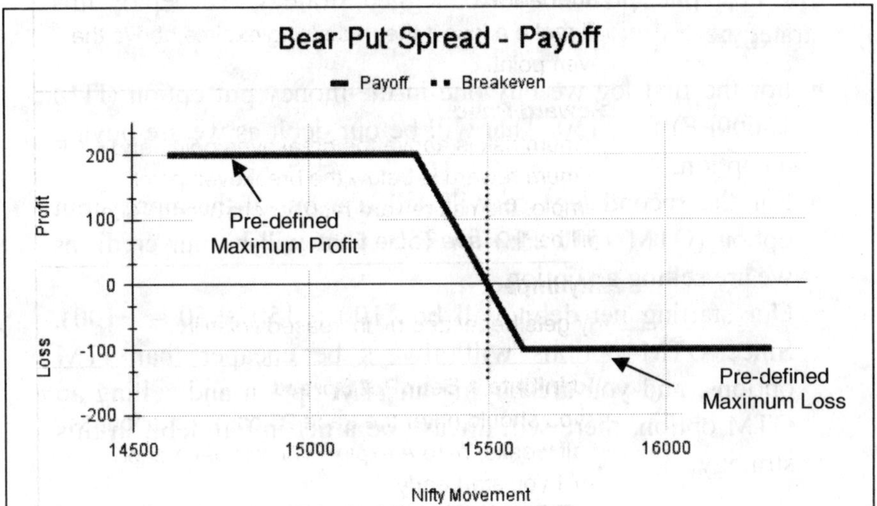

Figure 8.1: **Payoff Diagram of a Bear Put Spread**

Table 8.2

Our Hypothetical Nifty Bear Put Spread

Particular	*Value*
Underlying	Nifty
Spot Price	15,425
Buy ITM PE	15,600
Sell OTM PE	15,300
Debit from long put (₹)	−150
Credit from short put (₹)	50
Net debit (₹)	−150 + 50 = −100

Table 8.2 summarises the particulars of our hypothetical Nifty bear put spread trade.

Let us go over the trade particulars laid out in Table 8.2. We initiate our hypothetical trade with Nifty at 15425 spot levels. The bear put spread is a two-legged strategy. To deploy this strategy:

- For the first leg we buy one in-the-money put option (ITM 15600PE) for ₹150. That will be our debit as we are buying an option.
- For the second leg we will sell one out-of-the-money put option (OTM 15300PE) for ₹50. That will be our credit as we are selling an option.
- Our starting net debit will be ₹100 (−150 + 50 = −100). Since OTM options will always be cheaper than ITM options, and you are buying an ITM option and selling an OTM option, there will always be a net initial debit in this strategy.

Payoff Table

When the underlying Nifty moves in either direction, there will be a certain profit or loss. Table 8.3 illustrates the payoff, i.e. profit / loss, scenarios for various levels of Nifty expiry. For ease of understanding there is a 100-point difference between each hypothetical Nifty expiry.

Table 8.3

Payoff Table for Different Levels of Nifty Expiry

Market Expiry	*Long ITM PE Strike 15600 Intrinsic Value (₹)*	*Long ITM PE Strike 15600 Payoff (₹)*	*Short OTM PE Strike 15300 Intrinsic Value (₹)*	*Short OTM PE Strike 15300 Payoff (₹)*	*Strategy Payoff (₹)*	*Comments*
14,600	1,000	850	700	–650	200	
14,700	900	750	600	–550	200	
14,800	800	650	500	–450	200	
14,900	700	550	400	–350	200	Profit Zone. Maximum Profit Capped.
15,000	600	450	300	–250	200	
15,100	500	350	200	–150	200	
15,200	400	250	100	–50	200	
15,300	300	150	0	50	200	
15,400	200	50	0	50	100	
15,500	100	–50	0	50	0	Breakeven Point.
15,600	0	–150	0	50	–100	
15,700	0	–150	0	50	–100	
15,800	0	–150	0	50	–100	Loss Zone. Maximum Loss Capped.
15,900	0	–150	0	50	–100	
16,000	0	–150	0	50	–100	
16,100	0	–150	0	50	–100	

The breakeven point for this strategy will be:

ITM strike minus net debit.

This will translate to the Nifty level of 15600 − 100 = 15500. This means:

- If Nifty were to expire below 15500, you will make a pre-defined profit.
- Correspondingly, if Nifty expires above 15500, you will make a pre-defined loss.
- If Nifty expires at 15500 you will neither make a profit nor a loss as this is our breakeven point.

A bear put spread is similar to a bear call spread in terms of profit and loss scenarios — with one fundamental difference. Bear put spread is invoked for initial net debit. On the other hand, bear call spread is invoked for initial net credit. **We may prefer a bear call spread over a bear put spread when the market outlook is negative and option premiums are attractive enough to provide a good credit.**

How Greeks Impact the Payoff

Having grasped the payoff table for different Nifty expiries (Table 8.3), let's understand the relationship between the underlying's price movement and the various option Greeks for a bear put spread. We will not get into calculating the Greeks, but will focus instead on trying to understand how the various Greeks impact the payoff from this strategy.

Payoff *vis-à-vis* Delta

The long put option in a bear put spread, 15600PE in this case, has a negative Delta. This means that when the underlying's price falls, the value of the long put option will increase, resulting in a loss from the long put leg. The Delta of the long put option will typically be close to −1 for the ITM option, and will increase as the option moves further OTM.

The short put option in a bear put spread, 15300PE in this case, has a positive Delta. This means that as the price of the underlying asset falls, the value of the short put option also reduces, resulting in profit from this short put leg. The Delta of the short put option will typically be positive, and its value can approach +1 as it becomes more in-the-money (ITM).

The combination of a long put option with negative Delta, and a short put option having a positive Delta, creates an overall negative Delta in a bear put spread. This indicates that the overall position benefits from a fall in the underlying asset's price. **The strategy aims to profit from a downward move in the underlying asset's price, but it's not designed to profit from significant declines,** since the profit gets capped by the long put option leg.

Payoff *vis-à-vis* Gamma

The long put option in a bear put spread, 15600PE in this case, has a positive Gamma value. As the underlying asset's price falls, the Gamma of the long put option causes its Delta to become more sensitive to further price changes. This means that the long put option becomes more responsive to further falls in the underlying asset's price. This effect is beneficial for the strategy, as it enhances potential gains if the underlying asset's price falls.

The short put option in a bear put spread, 15300PE in this case, has a negative Gamma value. As the price of the underlying asset falls, the Gamma of the short put option causes its Delta to become more sensitive to further price changes. This means that the short put option becomes more responsive to further falls in the underlying asset's price. This effect is relatively stronger compared to the long put option's Gamma due to the lower strike price.

The combination of a long put option with a positive Gamma, and a short put option having negative Gamma, creates an overall positive Gamma in a bear put spread. This indicates that the overall position benefits from larger price movements in the underlying asset. As the underlying's price falls, the Delta of the overall position becomes more negative, potentially resulting in larger profits.

Payoff *vis-à-vis* Vega

The long put option in a bear put spread, 15600PE in this case, has a positive Vega. This means that any increase in implied volatility will generally increase the value of the long put option. Higher implied volatility in turn leads to higher option prices, which can result in potential gains for the long put option. Conversely, if implied volatility falls, the value of the long put option may also reduce, potentially leading to losses.

The short put option in a bear put spread, 15300PE in this case, has a negative Vega. This means that any rise in implied volatility will generally increase the value of the short put option. Higher implied volatility in turn leads to higher option prices, which can result in losses from the short put option. Conversely, if implied volatility reduces, the value of the short put option may fall, potentially leading to profits.

The combination of a long put option with a positive Vega and a short put option having a negative Vega creates an overall positive Vega in a bear put spread. This means that any increase in implied volatility will generally benefit the strategy.

On the other hand, a reduction in implied volatility may adversely affect the strategy's overall value.

Payoff *vis-à-vis* Theta

The long put option in a bear put spread, 15600PE in this case, has a negative Theta. This means that all else being equal, as time passes the value of the long put option will fall. The Theta of the long put option will typically be higher for options with shorter time to expiration. This time decay works against the strategy's potential profitability from the long put option component.

The short put option in a bear put spread, 15300PE in this case, has a positive Theta. This means that all else being equal, as time passes the value of the short put option will fall, resulting in profits from this leg. The Theta of the short put option will typically be higher for options with shorter time to expiration. This time decay works in favour of the strategy's potential profitability from the short put option.

The combination of a long put option with negative Theta and a short put option having positive Theta, creates an overall negative Theta for a bear put spread. This indicates that as the price of underlying moves further down towards the strike of the short put, the negative Theta reduces because the sold put provides more time decay benefits..

Over time, Theta has a direct impact on the bear put spread strategy's profitability. As time progresses, the strategy's value decreases due to the negative Theta. However, the limited profit potential and potential losses need to be considered. Traders should aim to close or adjust their position before expiration to capture available profits, as the strategy's profitability may diminish with approaching expiration.

Summary

In this chapter we have discussed:

- How and when the bear put spread strategy works profitably.
- What will be the payoff from it at different levels of the underlying asset's expiry.
- We also saw how Greeks impact the payoff from this strategy.

Let's go ahead to our next strategy.

9

Put Ratio Back Spread

THIS IS THE THIRD in our group of bearish strategies.

First we will review the put ratio back spread in a concise manner. Thereafter we will consider this strategy's payoff diagram and payoff table to enable you to visualize the various profit and loss scenarios for different market expiries. In the end we will review the effect of option Greeks on the put ratio back spread.

Put Ratio Back Spread in a Nutshell

Put ratio back spread can be profitably deployed when:

- Volatility is high;
- You are bearish on the market / underlying; and
- You expect the price to go down quickly.

The aim is to make big profits when the market goes down, while at the same time limiting your losses if the market were to go up sharply instead.

Table 9.1 encapsulates the put ratio back spread in a nutshell for you to get a quick fix on how it works.

Table 9.1

Put Ratio Back Spread in a Nutshell

When to Use Put Ratio Back Spread

When you are bearish on the market and think that it will fall quickly from its current levels.

Trade Setup

Put ratio back spread is a three-leg strategy comprising:

— Leg-1: Selling 1 ITM Put (PE);

— Legs-2 and 3: Buying 2 OTM Puts (PE).

Breakeven Point

There will be two points of no profits and no losses, or breakeven points, in this strategy — one, in case the underlying moves lower, and a second one if the underlying moves up.

Profit Scenarios

You will make profits if the underlying expires below the lower breakeven point. If the underlying expires above the higher breakeven point, the trader will still make nominal profits.

Loss Scenarios

You will make a loss if the underlying expires in between the lower and higher breakeven points.

Risk Reward Ratio

- The maximum risk (₹150) in our hypothetical trade is at 15300 (*see* Table 9.2), and
- The maximum reward is unlimited once the lower breakeven point is breached
- There is a limited reward above the higher breakeven point — ₹50 in our hypothetical trade (*see* Table 9.2).

Volatility Impact

Strategy gets benefitted by decreased volatility.

(Contd . . .)

Table 9.1: **Put Ratio Back Spread in a Nutshell** *(. . . contd.)*

	When to Initiate a Put Ratio Back Spread Ideally, you should enter the trade 25 days, i.e. about 3-and-a-half weeks, before expiry. You will get a good premium if you start early.
	When to Exit the Trade You should exit the trade: ▪ When market becomes stagnant and it may reverse from current levels, or ▪ The stop loss is hit, or ▪ One week before expiry, whichever event occurs first.

Payoff Diagram

Figure 9.1 is the payoff diagram for the put ratio back spread. As depicted by the payoff graph, while profits are unknown and could be unlimited, but losses are pre-defined for this strategy.

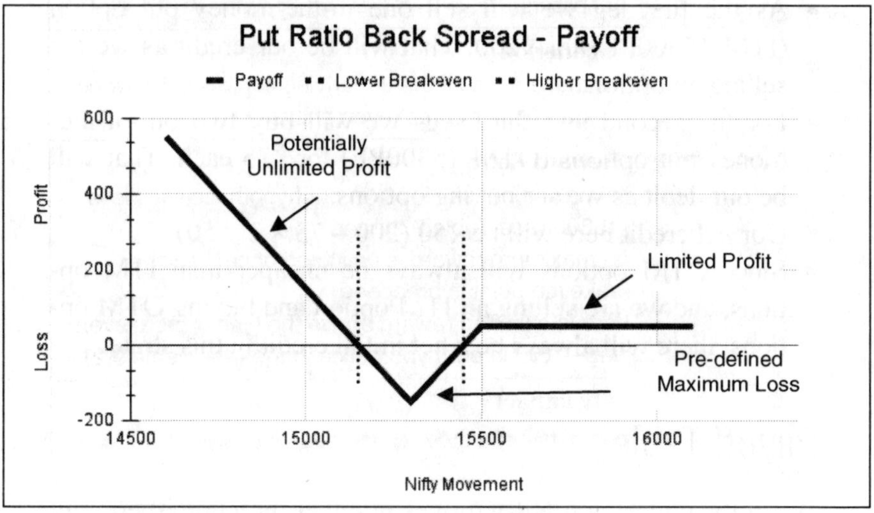

Figure 9.1: **Payoff Diagram for a Put Ratio Back Spread**

Table 9.2

Our Hypothetical Nifty Put Ratio Back Spread

Particular	*Value*
Underlying	Nifty
Spot Price	15425
Sell 1 ITM PE	15500
Buy 2 OTM PE	15300
Credit from selling option (₹)	200
Debit from buying options (₹)	−75 × 2= −150
Net Credit (₹)	200 − 75 × 2=50

Table 9.2 shows the particulars of our hypothetical Nifty trade. We are considering the example of a Nifty trade because Nifty is the most widely traded derivative in India.

The trade is initiated with Nifty at 15425 spot levels. To deploy this three-legged strategy:

- As the first leg we will sell one in-the-money put option (ITM 15500PE) for ₹200. That will be our credit as we are selling an option.
- For the second and third legs we will buy two out-of-the-money put options (OTM 15300PE) for ₹75 each. That will be our debit as we are buying options.
- Our net credit here will be ₹50 (200 – 75 × 2 = 50).
- Since OTM options will always be cheaper than ITM options, and we are selling an ITM option and buying OTM options, there will always be a net initial credit in this strategy.

Payoff Table

When the underlying Nifty moves in either direction, there will be a certain profit or loss. Table 9.3 illustrates the payoff, i.e.

profit / loss, scenarios for various levels of Nifty expiry. For ease of understanding there is a 100-point difference between each hypothetical Nifty expiry.

Table 9.3

Payoff Table for Different Levels of Nifty Expiry

Market Expiry	*Short ITM Strike 15500 Intrinsic Value (₹)*	*Short ITM Strike 15500 Payoff (₹)*	*Long OTM Strike 15300 Intrinsic Value (₹)*	*Long OTM Strike 15300 Payoff (₹)*	*Strategy Payoff (₹)*	*Comments*
14,600	900	–700	1,400	1,250	550	Profit Zone. Potentially Unlimited Profit.
14,700	800	–600	1,200	1,050	450	
14,800	700	–500	1,000	850	350	
14,900	600	–400	800	650	250	
15,000	500	–300	600	450	150	
15,100	400	–200	400	250	50	
15,150	350	–150	300	150	0	Breakeven Point.
15,200	300	–100	200	50	–50	Loss Zone. Maximum Loss Capped.
15,300	200	0	0	–150	–150	
15,400	100	100	0	–150	–50	
15,450	50	150	0	–150	0	Breakeven Point.
15,500	0	200	0	–150	50	Limited Profit Zone. Maximum Profit Capped.
15,600	0	200	0	–150	50	
15,700	0	200	0	–150	50	
15,800	0	200	0	–150	50	
15,900	0	200	0	–150	50	
16,000	0	200	0	–150	50	
16,100	0	200	0	–150	50	

From Table 9.3, you can see that lower and higher break-even points would be around 15150 and 15450, respectively. Accordingly:

- If Nifty expires below 15150 you will make good profits.
- If Nifty expires above 15450 you will still make nominal profits as shown by Table 9.3.
- If Nifty expires at around 15150 or 15450, you will neither make a profit nor end up with a loss as these two levels are the two breakeven points for our trade.
- If Nifty expires between 15150 and 15450 you will incur losses as revealed in Table 9.3 and Figure 9.1.

How Greeks Impact the Payoff

Having grasped the payoff table for different levels of Nifty expiry, let's understand the relationship between the underlying's price movement and various option Greeks for a put ratio back spread. We will not get into calculating the Greeks, but will focus instead on trying to understand how the various Greeks impact the payoff from this strategy.

Payoff *vis-à-vis* Delta

The short put option in a put ratio back spread, 15500PE in this case, has a positive Delta value. As the price of the underlying asset falls, the value of the short put option increases, resulting in profits from the strategy. The Delta of the short put option will typically be positive, and its value can approach +1 as it becomes more in-the-money (ITM).

The two long put options in a put ratio back spread, 15300PE in this case, have negative Delta values. As the price of the underlying asset falls, the value of the long put options increases, resulting in an adverse effect on the strategy. The Delta of the long put options will typically be negative, and their value can approach −1 as they become more in-the-money (ITM).

The put ratio back spread strategy involves the combination of a short put option having a positive Delta, and two long put options having negative Delta. The exact impact on Delta of the overall position depends on the ratio of short puts to long puts. Typically, the strategy benefits from a significant downward move in the underlying asset's price, but the profit potential may be limited if the downward price movement is not substantial or big enough.

Payoff *vis-à-vis* Gamma

The short put option in a put ratio back spread, 15500PE in this case, has a negative Gamma value. As the price of the underlying asset falls, the Gamma of the short put option causes its Delta to become more positive, potentially moving nearer to +1. This means that the short put option will becomes more sensitive to further falls in the underlying's price. This effect is beneficial for the strategy since it enhances the potential gains if the price of the underlying (Nifty) were to decline.

The long put options in a put ratio back spread, 15300PE in this case, have positive Gamma values. As the price of the underlying asset falls, the Gamma of the long put options causes their Delta to become more negative, potentially moving closer to −1. This means that the long put options become more sensitive to further falls in the underlying asset's price. This effect is relatively stronger compared to the Gamma of the short put option's due to the lower strike price.

In a put ratio back spread, the combination of a short put option having negative Gamma, and two long put options with positive Gamma, creates a mixed Gamma for the strategy. The overall Gamma effect on the strategy's payoff is determined by the specific ratio of the short put to long puts, and their respective strikes. Generally, this strategy benefits from larger price movements in the underlying asset, especially if its price moves significantly lower. In fact, the strategy aims to profit from a significant downward move in the underlying asset's price.

Payoff *vis-à-vis* Vega

The short put option in a put ratio back spread, 15500PE in this case, has a negative Vega. This means that any rise in implied volatility will generally lower the value of the short put option. Lower implied volatility in turn leads to lower option prices, which can result in potential gains for the short put option. Conversely, if the implied volatility rises, the value of the short put option may fall, potentially leading to losses.

The two long put options in a put ratio back spread, 15300PE in this case, have a positive Vega. This means that any rise in implied volatility will generally increase the value of the long put options. Lower implied volatility in turn leads to lower option prices, which can result in potential gains for the long put options. Conversely, if implied volatility rises, the value of the long put options may increase, potentially leading to losses.

The combination of a short put option, which has a negative Vega, and the two long put options having positive Vega creates an overall negative Vega for put ratio back spread. This means that any rise in implied volatility will generally affect the overall strategy adversely. Conversely, any fall in implied volatility may benefit the overall strategy. As the underlying asset's price changes, the impact of implied volatility changes on the short and long put options can affect the overall position.

Payoff *vis-à-vis* Theta

In a put ratio back spread the short put option, 15500PE in this case, has a positive Theta value. This means that all else being equal, as time passes the value of the short put option will increase. The Theta of the short put option will typically be higher for options with shorter time to expiration. This time decay works in favour of the strategy's potential profitability from the short put option.

The two long put options in a put ratio back spread, 15300PE in this case, have negative Theta values. This means that all else being equal, as time passes the values of the long put options will fall. The Theta of the long put options will also typically be higher for options with shorter time to expiration. This time decay thus adversely affects the strategy's potential profitability from the long put options.

The combination of a short put option having a positive Theta, and two long put options with negative Theta in a put ratio back spread creates an overall positive Theta for the trade position. This implies that as time passes, the strategy generally experiences time decay that contributes to its potential profitability. As time progresses, the values of both the short and long put options increase due to positive Theta.

Summary

In this chapter we have discussed:

- How the put ratio back spread strategy works.

- What will be the payoff from this strategy at different levels of market expiry.
- We also saw how the various Greeks impact the payoff from this strategy.

Let's now go ahead to our next strategy.

10

~

Bull Put Ladder

THIS IS THE FOURTH AND FINAL BEARISH STRATEGY covered in this book.

First we will see this strategy in a concise manner. Thereafter we will consider this strategy's payoff diagram and payoff table to enable you to visualize the various profit and loss scenarios for different market expiries. In the end, we will review the effect of option Greeks on a bull put ladder.

Bull Put Ladder in a Nutshell

The bull put ladder, is a strategy which you could deploy when:

- Volatility is high;
- You are bearish on the underlying; and
- You expect the price will head down quickly.

The goal is to make big profits when the market moves downwards, but at the same time you want to limit your losses in case the market rises sharply instead.

This strategy is an enhancement of the put ratio back spread and should be deployed when a trader is very confident that the market will move downwards from current levels.

Table 10.1 encapsulates this strategy in a nutshell, from start to end, for you to get a quick fix on how the bull put ladder works.

Table 10.1

Bull Put Ladder in a Nutshell

	When to Use Bull Put Ladder When you are very bearish and think that the price will move down quickly from its current levels.
	Trade Setup The bull put ladder is a three-leg strategy comprising: — Leg-1: Selling one ITM Put (PE); — Leg-2: Buying one ATM Put (PE); — Leg-3: Buying one OTM Put (PE).
	Breakeven Point There will be two points of no profits and no losses, i.e. two breakeven points, in this strategy — one, in case the underlying moves lower and the second when the underlying moves higher.
	Profit Scenarios You will make big profits if the underlying expires below the lower breakeven point. Even if the underlying expires above the higher breakeven point, you will still make some profits.
	Loss Scenarios You will make a loss if the underlying expires between the lower and higher breakeven points.
	Risk Reward Ratio ▪ Maximum risk is between two the breakeven points; it is ₹150 for our hypothetical trade (*see* Table 10.2). ▪ Maximum reward is unlimited once the lower breakeven point is breached. ▪ Reward is limited above the higher breakeven point — it is ₹50 in our hypothetical trade (*see* Table 10.2).

(Contd . . .)

Table 10.1: **Bull Put Ladder in a Nutshell** *(. . . contd.)*

	Volatility Impact Strategy gets benefitted by decreased volatility.
	Trade Initiation Ideally, you should enter the trade 25 days, i.e. about 3-and-a-half weeks, before expiry. You will get a good premium if you start early.
	When to Exit the Trade You should exit the trade: ▪ When market becomes stagnant and it may reverse from current levels, or ▪ The stop loss is hit, or ▪ One week before expiry, whichever event occurs first.

Payoff Diagram

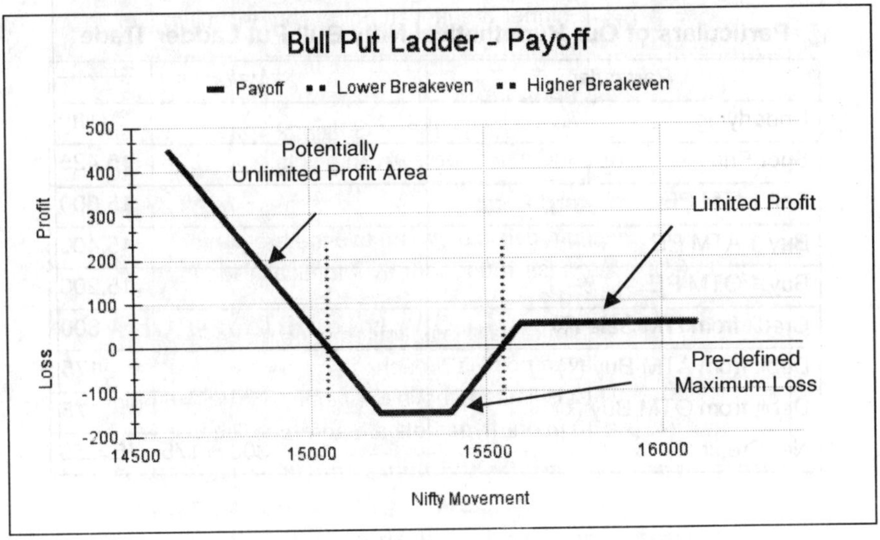

Figure 10.1: **Payoff Diagram for a Bull Put Ladder**

Figure 10.1 is the payoff diagram for the bull put ladder strategy. As depicted by the graph, while profits could be unlimited but losses for this strategy are pre-defined.

We will take the example of a Nifty trade here as it is the most widely traded derivative in India. Table 10.2 details the particulars of our hypothetical Nifty trade.

The hypothetical trade is initiated with Nifty at 15425 spot levels. As bull put ladder is a three-legged strategy, to deploy this strategy:

- For the first leg, we will sell one in-the-money put option (ITM 15600PE) for ₹300. That will be a credit as we are selling an option.
- For the second leg, we will buy one at-the-money put option (ATM 15400PE) for ₹175. That will be a debit as we are buying an option.

Table 10.2

Particulars of Our Hypothetical Nifty Bull Put Ladder Trade

Particular	*Value*
Underlying	Nifty
Spot Price	15,425
Sell 1 ITM PE	15,600
Buy 1 ATM PE	15,400
Buy 1 OTM PE	15,200
Credit from ITM Sale (₹)	300
Debit from ATM Buy (₹)	175
Debit from OTM Buy (₹)	75
Net Credit (₹)	300 – 175 –75 = 50

- For the third leg, we will buy one out-of-the-money put option (OTM 15200PE) for ₹75. That too will be a debit as we are again buying an option.
- Our net credit here will thus be ₹50 [300 − (175 + 75) = 50]. Since ATM and OTM options are cheaper than ITM options, and as we are selling an ITM option and buying ATM and OTM options, there will always be a net initial credit in this strategy.

Payoff Table

When the underlying Nifty moves in either direction, there will be a certain profit or loss. Table 10.3 illustrates the payoff, i.e. profit / loss, scenarios for various levels of Nifty expiry. For ease of understanding there is a 100-point difference between each hypothetical Nifty expiry.

From Table 10.3 you can see that the lower and higher break-even points would be around 15050 and 15550, respectively.

- If Nifty expires below 15050, you will make good profits.
- If Nifty expires above 15550, you will still make nominal profits as shown in Table 10.3.
- If Nifty expires at 15050 or 15550 you will neither make a profit nor lose money as these are our two breakeven points.
- If Nifty expires between 15050 and 15550, you will incur losses as shown both in the payoff table and graph.

Table 10.3

Payoff Table for Different Levels of Nifty Expiry

Market Expiry	*Short ITM Strike 15600 Intrinsic Value (₹)*	*Short ITM Strike 15600 Payoff (₹)*	*Long ATM Strike 15400 Intrinsic Value (₹)*	*Long ATM Strike 15400 Payoff (₹)*	*Long OTM Strike 15200 Intrinsic Value (₹)*	*Long OTM Strike 15200 Payoff (₹)*	*Strategy Payoff (₹)*	*Comments*
14,600	1,000	−700	800	625	600	525	450	Profit Zone. Potentially Unlimited Profit.
14,700	900	−600	700	525	500	425	350	
14,800	800	−500	600	425	400	325	250	
14,900	700	−400	500	325	300	225	150	
15,000	600	−300	400	225	200	125	50	
15,050	550	−250	350	175	150	75	0	Lower Breakeven Point.
15,100	500	−200	300	125	100	25	−50	Loss Zone. Max Loss Capped.
15,200	400	−100	200	25	0	−75	−150	
15,250	350	−50	150	−25	0	−75	−150	
15,300	300	0	100	−75	0	−75	−150	
15,350	250	50	50	−125	0	−75	−150	
15,400	200	100	0	−175	0	−75	−150	
15,500	100	200	0	−175	0	−75	−50	
15,550	50	250	0	−175	0	−75	0	Higher Breakeven Point.
15,600	0	300	0	−175	0	−75	50	Profit Zone. Maximum Profit Capped.
15,650	0	300	0	−175	0	−75	50	
15,700	0	300	0	−175	0	−75	50	
15,750	0	300	0	−175	0	−75	50	
15,800	0	300	0	−175	0	−75	50	
15,900	0	300	0	−175	0	−75	50	
16,000	0	300	0	−175	0	−75	50	
16,100	0	300	0	−175	0	−75	50	

How Greeks Impact the Payoff

Having grasped the payoff table for different Nifty expiries, let's understand the relationship between the underlying's price movement and various option Greeks for this strategy. We will not be getting into calculating the Greeks, but will focus instead on trying to understand how the various Greeks impact the payoff from this strategy.

Payoff *vis-à-vis* Delta

The short put option in a bull put ladder — 15600PE in this case — has a positive Delta value. As the price of the underlying asset falls, the value of the short put option decreases, benefiting the strategy. The Delta of the short put option will typically be positive and their value can approach +1 as it becomes more in-the-money (ITM).

The two long put options in a bull put ladder, 15400PE and 15200PE in our hypothetical trade, have negative Delta values. As the price of the underlying asset falls, the values of the long put options increase, resulting in losses from these two legs. The Delta of a long put option will typically be negative and its value can approach −1 as it becomes more in-the-money (ITM).

The bull put ladder strategy involves the combination of a short put option, having a positive Delta, and two long put options having negative Delta. The exact impact on the overall Delta position depends on the ratio of the short put to long puts. The strategy typically benefits from a significant downward move in the underlying asset's price, but it may have limited profit potential if the price movement is not substantial enough.

Payoff *vis-à-vis* Gamma

In a bull put ladder, the short put option, 15600PE in this case, has a negative Gamma value. As the price of the underlying asset falls, the Gamma of the short put option causes the Delta to become more positive, potentially moving closer to +1. This means that the short put option becomes more sensitive to further falls in the price of the underlying. This effect is beneficial for the strategy, as it enhances potential gains if the underlying asset's price declines.

The long put options in a bull put ladder, 15400PE and 15200PE in this case, have positive Gamma values. As the price of the underlying asset falls, the Gamma of the long put options causes their Delta to become more negative, potentially moving closer to −1. This means that the long put options become more sensitive to further falls in the underlying asset's price. This effect is relatively stronger compared to the Gamma of the short put option due to a lower strike price.

In a bull put ladder the combination of a short put option having negative Gamma, and two long put options with positive Gamma creates an overall mixed Gamma for the strategy. The overall effect of Gamma on the strategy's payoff is determined by the specific ratio of the short put to long puts, and their respective strikes. Generally, the strategy benefits from larger price moves in the underlying asset, especially if it moves significantly lower. A bull put ladder aims to profit from a significant downward move in the underlying asset's price.

Payoff *vis-à-vis* Vega

The short put option in a bull put ladder, 15600PE in this case, has a negative Vega. This means that any increase in implied volatility will generally increase the value of the short put option, resulting in a loss from this leg. On the other hand, lower implied volatility leads to lower option prices, which can result in potential gains for the short put option.

In a bull put ladder the long put options, 15400PE and 15200PE in this case, have a positive Vega. This means that any rise in implied volatility will generally increase the value of the long put options, which can result in potential gains from the long put legs.

In a bull put ladder the combination of a short put option with negative Vega, and two long put options having positive Vega creates an overall negative Vega for the strategy. This means that any increase in implied volatility will generally adversely affect the overall strategy. Conversely, a fall in implied volatility may benefit the overall strategy. As the underlying asset's price moves, the impact of changes in implied volatility on the short and long put options can affect the overall position.

Payoff *vis-à-vis* Theta

In a bull put ladder the short put option, 15600PE in this case, has a positive Theta value. This means that as time passes, all else being equal the value of the short put option will fall resulting in benefits from this leg. The Theta of a short put option will typically be higher for an option with shorter time to expiration. This time decay works in favour of the strategy's potential profitability from the short put option.

Conversely, in a bull put ladder the two long put options, 15400PE and 15200PE in this case, have negative Theta values. Thus, as time passes, all else being equal the value of the long put options will fall. The Theta of the long put options will also typically be higher for options with shorter time to expiration. This time decay adversely contributes to the strategy's potential profitability from the long put option side.

In a bull put ladder, the combination of a short put option with positive Theta, and two long put options having negative

Theta creates an overall positive Theta for the strategy. This means that as time passes the strategy generally experiences time decay that contributes to its potential profitability.

Summary

In this chapter we have discussed:

- How the bull put ladder strategy works.
- What will be the payoff from it for different of expiry levels of the underlying.
- We also saw how Greeks will impact the payoff from the bull put ladder strategy.

With this we have concluded our bearish strategies and we now move on to the next section of the book which covers neutral strategies.

Part 3

~

Neutral or Delta Neutral Strategies

— for When You Expect the Price Will Remain Sideways!

11

~

Long Straddle

THIS IS THE FIRST OF THE DELTA NEUTRAL STRATEGIES presented in this book.

First we will review this strategy in a concise manner. Thereafter we will consider the long straddle's payoff diagram and payoff table for you to visualize the various profit and loss scenarios for different market expiries. Finally we will review the effect of options Greeks on a long straddle.

Long Straddle in a Nutshell

Long straddle is a strategy which you can deploy when:

- The market / underlying's volatility is high.
- You are not sure how the market will move in the next few trading sessions.
- You want to make a decent profit, irrespective of whether the market moves up or down.

Table 11.1 encapsulates this strategy in a nutshell, from start to end, for you to get a quick fix on how the long straddle works.

Table 11.1

Long Straddle in a Nutshell

	When to Use a Long Straddle If you are neutral on the market and unsure whether the market / underlying asset will move up or go down from its current levels.
	Trade Setup Long straddle is a two-leg strategy comprising: — Leg-1: Buying one ATM Call (CE); — Leg-2: Buying one ATM Put (PE).
	Breakeven Point There will be two points of no profits and no losses, i.e. two breakeven points in this strategy — one, when the underlying's price moves lower and another in case the underlying moves higher.
	Profit Scenarios You will make profits if the underlying expires above the higher breakeven point, or if it expires below the lower breakeven point.
	Loss Scenarios You will make a loss if the underlying expires between the two breakeven points.
	Risk Reward Ratio ▪ Maximum risk lies in between the two breakeven points; it is ₹325 at 15,400 level for our hypothetical trade (*see* Table 11.2), and ▪ Maximum reward is unlimited.
	Volatility Impact Strategy gets benefitted by increased volatility.
	When to Initiate the Trade Ideally you should enter the trade 25 days, namely about 3-and-a- half weeks, ahead of expiry. You will get a good premium if you start early.

(Contd . . .)

Table 11.1: **Long Straddle in a Nutshell** *(. . . contd.)*

	**When to Exit the Trade** You should exit the trade: ▪ When market becomes stagnant and volatility is decreasing, or ▪ The stop loss is hit, or ▪ One week before expiry, whichever event occurs first.

Payoff Diagram

As depicted by the graph in the payoff diagram (Figure 11.1), the long straddle strategy has a limited risk of loss but unlimited profit potential.

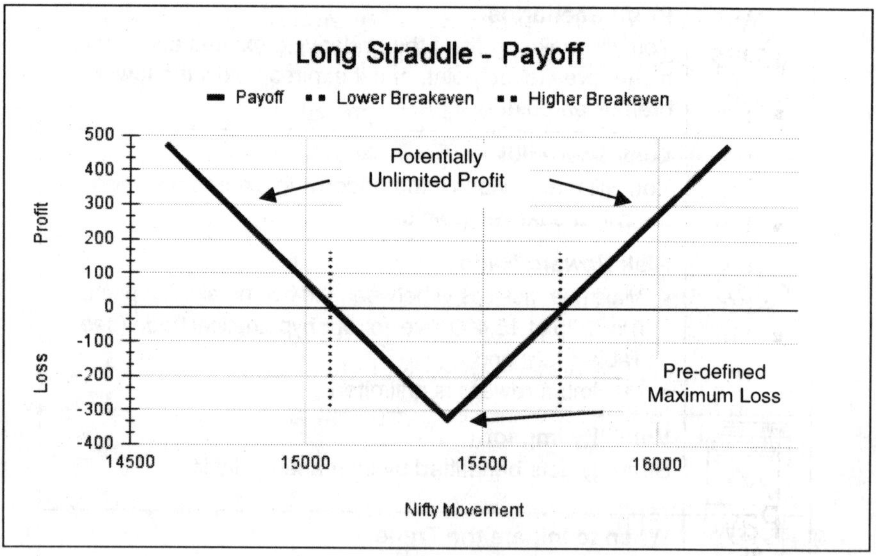

Figure 11.1: **Payoff Diagram for a Long Straddle**

Table 11.2

Particulars of Our Hypothetical Nifty Long Straddle

Particular	*Value*
Underlying	Nifty
Spot Price	15,425
Buy ATM CE	15,400
Buy ATM PE	15,400
Debit from buying call (₹)	−175
Debit from buying put (₹)	−150
Net Debit (₹)	−175 −150 = −325

We will consider the example of a hypothetical Nifty long straddle trade here as Nifty is the most widely traded derivative in India (Table 11.2).

We initiate our hypothetical long straddle trade with Nifty at 15425 spot levels. To deploy this two-legged strategy,

- For the first leg we will buy one at-the-money call option (ATM 15400CE) for ₹175. That will be our debit as we are buying an option.
- For the second leg we will buy one at-the-money put option (ATM 15400PE) for ₹150. That will also be a debit as we are again buying an option.
- Our net debit here will be ₹325 (175 + 150). Since we are buying ATM options there will always be an initial net debit in this strategy.

Payoff Table

When the underlying Nifty moves in either direction, there will be a certain profit or loss. Table 11.3 illustrates the payoff, i.e. profit / loss, scenarios for various levels of Nifty expiry. For

ease of understanding there is a 100-point difference between each hypothetical Nifty expiry.

Table 11.3

Payoff Table for Different Levels of Nifty Expiry

Market Expiry	*Long ATM CE Strike 15400 Intrinsic Value (₹)*	*Long ATM CE Strike 15400 Payoff (₹)*	*Long ATM PE Strike 15400 Intrinsic Value (₹)*	*Long ATM PE Strike 15400 Payoff (₹)*	*Strat-egy Payoff (₹)*	*Comments*
14,600	0	−175	800	650	475	Rising Profit Zone. Potentially Unlimited Profit.
14,700	0	−175	700	550	375	
14,800	0	−175	600	450	275	
14,900	0	−175	500	350	175	
15,000	0	−175	400	250	75	
15,075	0	-175	325	175	0	Lower Breakeven Point.
15,100	0	−175	300	150	−25	Loss Zone.
15,200	0	−175	200	50	−125	
15,300	0	−175	100	−50	−225	
15,400	0	−175	0	−150	−325	
15,500	100	−75	0	−150	−225	
15,600	200	25	0	−150	−125	
15,700	300	125	0	−150	−25	
15,725	325	150	0	-150	0	Higher Breakeven Point.
15,800	400	225	0	−150	75	Rising Profit Zone. Potentially Unlimited Profit.
15,900	500	325	0	−150	175	
16,000	600	425	0	−150	275	
16,100	700	525	0	−150	375	
16,200	800	625	0	−150	475	

From Table 11.3 you can see that lower and higher breakeven points would be around 15075 and 15725, respectively.

- If Nifty expires below 15075, you will make good profits.
- Similarly, if Nifty expires above 15725 you will again be in good profits as shown in the Table 11.3.
- If Nifty expires at 15075, or at 15725, you will neither make a profit nor a loss as this is our breakeven point.
- If Nifty expires between the two breakeven points, you will make a loss, as shown in the payoff table and the corresponding graph in Figure 11.1.

How Greeks Impact the Payoff

Having grasped the payoff for different Nifty expiries, let's consider the relationship between the underlying's price movement and various option Greeks for the long straddle. We will not get into calculating the Greeks, but will focus instead on trying to understand how the various Greeks impact the payoff from this strategy.

Payoff *vis-à-vis* Delta

The call option in a long straddle, 15400CE in this case, has a positive Delta value. As the price of the underlying asset rises, the value of the call option also increases. The Delta of the call option will typically be positive, and its value can approach +1 as it becomes more in-the-money (ITM).

The put option in a long straddle, 15400PE in this case, has a negative Delta value. As the price of the underlying Nifty falls, the value of the put option increases. The Delta of the put option will typically be negative, and its value can approach −1 as it becomes more in-the-money (ITM).

The combination of a call option, with a positive Delta, and a put option having a negative Delta in a long straddle creates an overall position with a relatively neutral Delta. This means that the strategy is less sensitive to small price movements in the underlying asset and grows more sensitive when the price moves significantly in either direction.

The long straddle strategy aims to profit from significant price moves in the underlying asset. If the price does move significantly in either direction, one of the options will become in-the-money (ITM), offsetting the loss from the other option. **The potential for profit is theoretically unlimited if the price moves far enough in one direction.**

Payoff *vis-à-vis* Gamma

The call option in a long straddle, 15400CE in this case, has a positive Gamma value. As the price of the underlying asset moves away from the strike price, whether up or down, the Gamma of the call option causes its Delta to become more sensitive to further price changes. This means that the call option's Delta will increase as the price moves further in-the-money (ITM), or further out-of-the-money (OTM).

The put option in a long straddle, 15400PE in this case, also has a positive Gamma value. As the underlying asset's price moves away from the strike price, whether up or down, the Gamma of the put option causes its Delta to become more sensitive to further price changes. This means that the put option's Delta will increase as the price moves further in-the-money (ITM) or further out-of-the-money (OTM).

The combination of a call option with positive Gamma, and a put option having positive Gamma in a long straddle creates an overall high Gamma position. This indicates that the strategy becomes more sensitive to price changes as the underlying asset's price moves away from the strike price in either direction.

Payoff *vis-à-vis* Vega

In a long straddle the call option, 15400CE in this case, has a positive Vega value. This means that any increase in implied volatility will generally raise the value of the call option. Higher implied volatility in turn leads to higher option prices, potentially resulting in greater profits for the long call option. Conversely, any fall in implied volatility may lower the value of this leg.

The long put option in a long straddle, 15400PE in this case, also has a positive Vega value. Similar to the call option, any rise in implied volatility will also generally increase the value of the put option. Greater implied volatility, in turn, leads to higher option prices, potentially resulting in greater profits for the put option leg. Conversely, any reduction in implied volatility may lower the value of the put option.

In a long straddle, the combination of the long call option with a positive Vega, and the long put option also having a positive Vega creates an overall position with a relatively high positive Vega. This means that any increase in implied volatility will generally benefit the long straddle strategy by increasing the value of both call and put options. Conversely, a reduction in implied volatility may adversely affect the strategy's profitability.

Payoff *vis-à-vis* Theta

The long call option in a long straddle, 15400CE in this case, has a negative Theta value. This means that all else being equal, as time passes the value of the call option leg will fall. The Theta of the call option will typically be higher for options with shorter time to expiration. This time decay works against the strategy's potential profitability from the call option.

The long put option in a long straddle, 15400PE in this case, also has a negative Theta value. Similar to the call option, as time passes the value of the put option will also fall. The Theta of the put option will also typically be higher for options with shorter time to expiration. The time decay also works against the strategy's potential profitability from the put option.

The combination of a call option with a negative Theta and a put option having a negative Theta in a long straddle creates an overall position with a relatively high negative Theta. This means that as time passes, the strategy generally experiences time decay, and that can erode its potential profitability. However, the strategy's profitability depends on the magnitude of the underlying's price movement. Traders should, therefore, carefully consider the timing of their entry into this strategy and the potential magnitude of the price movement required to over-come the adverse effect of time decay and generate a profit.

Summary

In this chapter we have discussed:

- How a long straddle works.
- What the payoff from it would be at different expiry levels.
- We also saw how Greeks impact the payoff from this strategy.

On, now, to our next delta neutral strategy.

12

~

Short Straddle

SHORT STRADDLE IS THE SECOND NEUTRAL STRATEGY presented in this book.

First we will review this strategy in a concise manner. Thereafter we will consider the short straddle's payoff diagram and payoff table for you to visualize the various profit and loss scenarios at different market expiries. Finally, we will review the impact of option Greeks on a short straddle.

Short Straddle in a Nutshell

Short straddle is a strategy which you can deploy when:

- Market volatility is low;
- You believe that the market will not move much in either direction till the upcoming expiry.

Thus, you can use a short straddle when you want to make a decent profit in low volatility conditions where the market is only moving sideways and there is no clear trend in the market, whether up or down.

Table 12.1 encapsulates the short straddle in a nutshell, from start to end, for you to get a quick fix on how it works.

Table 12.1

Short Straddle in a Nutshell

	When to Use a Short Straddle You can use short straddle if you have a neutral view on the market and believe that there will not be any big upward or downward movement until the upcoming expiry.
	Trade Setup Short straddle is two-leg strategy comprising: — Leg-1: Selling one ATM Call (CE) — Leg-2: Selling one ATM Put (PE).
	Breakeven Point There will be two points of no profits and no losses or breakeven points in this strategy — one, when the underlying's price moves down, and another when the underlying's price moves higher.
	Profit Scenarios You will make profits if the underlying expires between the two breakeven points.
	Loss Scenarios You will make losses if the underlying expires above the higher breakeven point, or if the underlying expires below the lower breakeven point.
	Risk Reward Ratio ▪ Maximum risk is unlimited, and ▪ Maximum reward (₹325) is at 15,400 in our hypothetical trade (*see* Table 12.2).
	Volatility Impact Strategy gets benefitted by decreased volatility.

(Contd . . .)

Table 12.1: **Short Straddle in a Nutshell** *(. . . contd.)*

	When to Initiate the Trade Ideally you should enter the trade 25 days, namely about 3-and-a-half weeks, ahead of expiry. You will get a good premium if you start early.
	When to Exit the Trade You should exit the trade: ▪ When market started trending in either direction and volatility is increasing, or ▪ The stop loss is hit, or ▪ One week before expiry, whichever event occurs first.

Payoff Diagram

Figure 12.1 depicts the payoff diagram for a short straddle. As depicted by the graph, while this strategy offers a limited profit potential but there is risk of potentially unlimited loss.

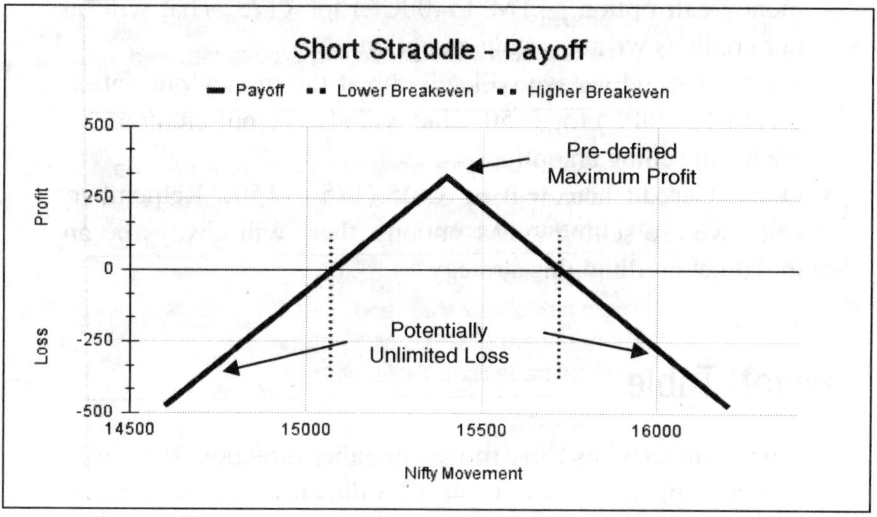

Figure 12.1: **Payoff Diagram for a Short Straddle**

Table 12.2

Our Hypothetical Nifty Short Straddle

Particular	*Value*
Underlying	Nifty
Spot Price (₹)	15425
Sell ATM CE	15400
Sell ATM PE	15400
Credit from selling call (₹)	175
Credit from selling put (₹)	150
Net Credit (₹)	175 + 150 = 325

We have used a hypothetical example of a Nifty trade here as Nifty is the most widely traded derivative in India. Table 12.2 details the particulars of our hypothetical Nifty trade.

The trade is initiated with Nifty at 15425 spot levels.

- For the first leg of our short straddle, we will sell one at-the-money call option (ATM 15400CE) for ₹175. That will be our credit as we are selling an option.
- For the second leg we will sell one at-the-money put option (ATM 15400PE) for ₹150. That will also be our credit as we are again selling an option.
- Our net credit here will be ₹325 (175 + 150). Remember, since we are selling ATM options, there will always be an initial net credit in this strategy.

Payoff Table

When the underlying Nifty moves in either direction, there will be a certain profit or loss. Table 12.3 illustrates the payoff, i.e. profit / loss, scenarios for various levels of Nifty expiry. For

ease of understanding there is a 100-point difference between each hypothetical Nifty expiry.

Table 12.3

Payoff Table for Different Levels of Nifty Expiry

Market Expiry	*Short ATM CE Strike 15400 Intrinsic Value (₹)*	*Short ATM CE Strike 15400 Payoff (₹)*	*Short ATM PE Strike 15400 Intrinsic Value (₹)*	*Short ATM PE Strike 15400 Payoff (₹)*	*Strategy Payoff (₹)*	*Comments*
14,600	0	175	800	−650	−475	Unlimited Loss Zone.
14,700	0	175	700	−550	−375	
14,800	0	175	600	−450	−275	
14,900	0	175	500	−350	−175	
15,000	0	175	400	−250	−75	
15,075	0	175	325	−175	0	Lower Breakeven Point.
15,100	0	175	300	−150	25	Profit Zone.
15,200	0	175	200	−50	125	
15,300	0	175	100	50	225	
15,400	0	175	0	150	325	
15,500	100	75	0	150	225	
15,600	200	−25	0	150	125	
15,700	300	−125	0	150	25	
15,725	325	−150	0	150	0	Higher Breakeven Point.
15,800	400	−225	0	150	−75	Unlimited Loss Zone.
15,900	500	−325	0	150	−175	
16,000	600	−425	0	150	−275	
16,100	700	−525	0	150	−375	
16,200	800	−625	0	150	−475	

From the payoff table you can see that the lower and higher breakeven points would be 15075 and 15725, respectively.

- You will incur a loss if Nifty expires below 15075.
- If Nifty expires above 15725 you will again be in a loss, as shown in Table 12.3.
- If Nifty expires at 15075 or 15725, you will neither make a profit nor lose money as these are our two breakeven points.
- If Nifty expires between the two breakeven points, you will make a profit through this strategy, as shown in the payoff table and the corresponding graph.

How Greeks Impact the Payoff

Having grasped the payoff table for different Nifty expiries, let's understand the relationship between the price movement and various option Greeks for this strategy. We will not get into calculating the Greeks, but will focus instead on trying to understand how the various Greeks impact the payoff in the case of a short straddle.

Payoff *vis-à-vis* Delta

In a short straddle, the call option (15400CE in this case) has a negative Delta value. As the price of the underlying asset rises, the value of the short call option falls. The Delta of the short call option will typically be negative, and its value can approach −1 as it grows more in-the-money (ITM).

In a short straddle the put option (15400PE in this case) has a positive Delta value. As the price of the underlying rises, the value of the short put option also increases. The Delta of the short put option will typically be positive, and its value can approach +1 as it becomes more in-the-money (ITM).

The combination of a short call option with negative Delta, and a short put option having positive Delta, creates an overall Delta neutral position for a short straddle. This means that the strategy is relatively neutral to small price movements in the underlying asset.

In fact, the short straddle strategy aims to profit from flat, i.e. sideways, price movement in the underlying asset. The strategy generates income from the premiums received for selling both the call and put options. **Due to the short call and put options, the risk is potentially unlimited both on the upside and downside.**

Payoff *vis-à-vis* Gamma

In a short straddle, the short call option (15400CE in this case) has a negative Gamma value. As the underlying's price moves away from the strike price, whether up or down, the Gamma of the short call option causes its Delta to become more sensitive to further price changes. This means that the call option's Delta will fall as the price moves further in-the-money (ITM) or further out-of-the-money (OTM).

The short put option in a short straddle (15400PE in this case) also has a negative Gamma value. Similar to the what happens in the case for short call option, as the price of the underlying asset moves away from the strike price — whether up or down — the Gamma of the short put option causes its Delta to become more sensitive to further price changes. This means that the put option's Delta will fall as the price moves further in-the-money (ITM) or further out-of-the-money (OTM).

The combination of a short call option having a negative Gamma, and a short put option also having a negative Gamma, creates an overall high negative Gamma for the short straddle. The short straddle position thus grows more sensitive to price changes as the underlying asset's price moves away from the strike price in either direction. The strategy's Gamma is highest when the underlying's price is close to the strike price.

Payoff *vis-à-vis* Vega

In a short straddle the short call option, 15400CE in this case, has a negative Vega value. This means that any rise in implied volatility will generally increase the value of the short call option, potentially resulting in greater losses from the short call option. Conversely, any reduction in implied volatility may lower the value of the short call option.

The short put option in a short straddle, 15400PE in this case, also has a negative Vega value. Similar to the case of the short call option, any rise in implied volatility will generally increase the value of the short put option, potentially resulting in greater losses from the short put option. Conversely, a fall in implied volatility may lower the value of the short put option.

In a short straddle, the combination of a short call option with a negative Vega and a short put option also having a negative Vega creates a trade position with an overall relatively high negative Vega. This means that any increase in implied volatility will adversely affect the overall strategy.

Payoff *vis-à-vis* Theta

In a short straddle, the short call option (15400CE in this case) has a positive Theta value. This means that all else being equal, as time passes the value (price) of the short call option will fall. The time decay works in favour of the strategy's potential profitability from the short call option.

The short put option in a short straddle (15400PE in this case) also has a positive Theta value. Similar to the case for the short call option, with the passage of time the value of the short put option will also fall. The time decay also works in favour of the strategy's potential profitability from the short put option.

In a short straddle the combination of a short call option with a positive Theta, and a short put option also having a positive Theta creates a position with an overall relatively high positive Theta. This means that as time passes, time decay can contribute to the short straddle's potential profitability. However, the strategy's profitability depends crucially on the magnitude of price movement. Over time, Theta has a direct impact on the short straddle strategy's profitability. Traders should therefore carefully consider the timing of their entry as highlighted in Table 12.1, and the potential magnitude of price movement required to overcome time decay and generate a profit.

Summary

In this chapter we have discussed:

- How the short straddle strategy works.
- What the payoff from it will be at different levels of market expiry.
- We also saw how Greeks impact the payoff from a short straddle.

Let's move on to our next strategy.

13

~

Long Strangle

THIS IS THE THIRD NEUTRAL STRATEGY which we will examine. First we will see how the long strangle strategy works in a concise manner. Thereafter we will consider its payoff diagram and payoff table to enable you to visualize the various profit and loss scenarios for different market expiries. Finally, we will review the impact of option Greeks on a long strangle.

Long Straggle in a Nutshell

Long strangle is a strategy which you can deploy when:

- Market volatility is high.
- You are not sure which way the market will move in the next few trading sessions.
- The goal is to make a decent profit, irrespective of the direction of the price movement, whether up or down.

Long strangle is an enhancement of the long straddle strategy. In a long straddle, a trader needs to buy ATM call and put options, while in a long strangle one buys OTM call and put options. Since OTM options are invariably cheaper than ATM options, long strangles are always cheaper to implement than long straddles.

Table 13.1 encapsulates the long strangle strategy in a nutshell, from start to end, for you to get a quick fix on how it works.

Table 13.1

Long Strangle in a Nutshell

	When to Use a Long Strangle When you have a neutral view on the market / underlying and are not sure whether it will move up or go down from its current levels.
	Trade Setup Long strangle is a two-leg strategy comprising: — Leg-1: Buying one OTM Call (CE); — Leg-2: Buying one OTM Put (PE).
	Breakeven Point There will be two points of no profits and no losses, i.e. two breakeven points, in this strategy – one, in case the underlying moves down, and another in case the underlying's price moves up.
	Profit Scenarios You will make profits if the underlying expires either above the higher breakeven point, or below the lower breakeven point.
	Loss Scenarios You will make a loss if the underlying expires in between two the breakeven points.
	Risk Reward Ratio ▪ Maximum risk (₹200) is between 15200 to 15700 levels in our hypothetical trade (*see* Table 13.2), while ▪ Maximum reward is unlimited.
	Volatility Impact Strategy gets benefitted by increased volatility.

(Contd . . .)

Table 13.1: **Long Strangle in a Nutshell** *(. . . contd.)*

	When to Initiate the Trade Ideally one should enter the trade 25 days, i.e. about 3 and a half weeks ahead of expiry. You will get a good premium when you start early.
	When to Exit the Trade You should exit the trade: ▪ When market becomes stagnant and volatility is decreasing, or ▪ The stop loss is hit, or ▪ One week before expiry, whichever event occurs first.

Payoff Diagram

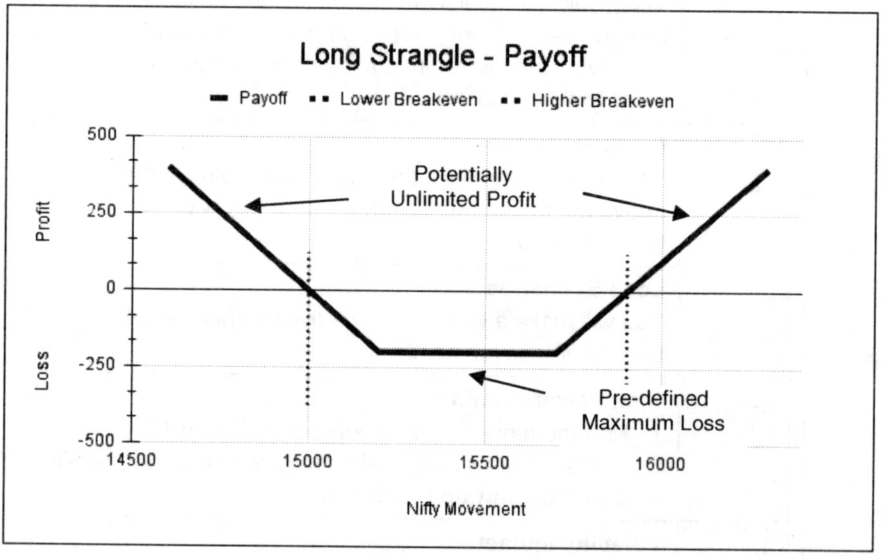

Figure 13.1: **Payoff Diagram for Long Strangle**

Figure 13.1 illustrates the payoff diagram for a long strangle. As depicted by the graph, this strategy puts a cap on how much you could lose but has unlimited profit potential.

We will use the example of a hypothetical Nifty trade, the most widely traded derivative in India. Table 13.2 highlights the particulars of our hypothetical Nifty trade using a long strangle.

We initiate our hypothetical trade with Nifty at 15425 spot levels. Long strangle being a two-legged strategy:

- For the first leg we will buy one out-of-the-money call option (OTM 15700CE) for ₹100. That will be our debit as we are buying an option.
- For the second leg we will buy one out-of-the-money put option (OTM 15200PE) for ₹100. That will also be our debit as we are buying an option.
- Our net debit here will be ₹200 (100 + 100). Since we are buying OTM options there will always be a net initial debit in a long strangle.

Table 13.2

Particulars of Our Hypothetical Nifty Long Strangle

Particular	*Value*
Underlying	Nifty
Spot Price	15,425
Buy OTM CE	15,700
Buy OTM PE	15,200
Debit from buying call (₹)	−100
Debit from buying put (₹)	−100
Net Debit (₹)	−100 −100 = −200

Payoff Table

When the underlying Nifty moves in either direction, there will be a certain profit or loss. Table 13.3 illustrates the payoff, i.e.

Table 13.3

Payoff Table for Different Levels of Nifty Expiry

Market Expiry	*Long OTM CE Strike 15700 Intrinsic Value (₹)*	*Long OTM CE Strike 15700 Payoff (₹)*	*Long OTM PE Strike 15200 Intrinsic Value (₹)*	*Long OTM PE Strike 15200 Payoff (₹)*	*Strategy Payoff (₹)*	*Comments*
14,600	0	−100	600	500	400	Rising Profit Zone.
14,700	0	−100	500	400	300	
14,800	0	−100	400	300	200	
14,900	0	−100	300	200	100	
15,000	0	−100	200	100	0	Lower Breakeven Point.
15,100	0	−100	100	0	−100	Loss Zone. Maximum Loss Capped.
15,200	0	−100	0	−100	−200	
15,300	0	−100	0	−100	−200	
15,400	0	−100	0	−100	−200	
15,500	0	−100	0	−100	−200	
15,600	0	−100	0	−100	−200	
15,700	0	−100	0	−100	−200	
15,800	100	0	0	−100	−100	
15,900	200	100	0	−100	0	Higher Breakeven Point.
16,000	300	200	0	−100	100	Rising Profit Zone.
16,100	400	300	0	−100	200	
16,200	500	400	0	−100	300	
16,300	600	500	0	−100	400	

profit / loss, scenarios for various levels of Nifty expiry. For ease of understanding there is a 100-point difference between each hypothetical Nifty expiry.

From Table 13.3, you can see that the lower and higher breakeven points are at 15000 and 15900, respectively.

- If Nifty expires below 15000 you will make good profits.
- If Nifty expires above 15900 you will again be in good profits as shown in the payoff Table 13.3.
- If Nifty expires at either 15000 or 15900, you will make neither a profit nor a loss as these are the trade's breakeven points.
- If Nifty expires in between the two breakeven points, you will make a loss using this strategy as shown in the payoff table and corresponding graph.

How Greeks Impact the Payoff

Having grasped the payoff table for different Nifty expiries in Table 13.3, let's understand the relationship between the underlying's price movement and the various option Greeks for this strategy. We will not get into calculating the Greeks, but will focus instead on trying to understand how the various Greeks impact the payoff from a long strangle trade.

Payoff *vis-à-vis* Delta

In a long strangle, the call option (15700CE in this case) has a positive Delta value. Thus, as the underlying asset's price rises, the value of the call option also increases. The Delta of the call option will typically be positive, and its value can approach +1 as it becomes more in-the-money (ITM).

The put option in a long strangle (15200PE in this case) has a negative Delta value. Accordingly, as the price of the underlying asset falls, the value of the put option increases. The Delta of the put option will typically be negative, and its value can approach −1 as it grows more in-the-money (ITM).

In a long strangle the combination of a call option with a positive Delta, and a put option having negative Delta, creates an overall position which has relatively neutral Delta. This means that the strategy is less sensitive to small price movements in the underlying asset, but grows more sensitive as the price moves significantly in either direction.

The long strangle strategy aims to profit from significant price movements in the underlying asset. If the price moves significantly in either direction, one of the options will become in-the-money (ITM), offsetting the loss from the other option leg. The potential for profit is theoretically unlimited if the price moves far enough in any direction.

Payoff *vis-à-vis* Gamma

In a long strangle, the call option (15700CE in this case) has a positive Gamma value. As the price of the underlying asset moves away from the strike price in either direction, the Gamma of the call option causes its Delta to become more sensitive to further price changes. This means that the call option's Delta will rise as the price moves further whether in-the-money (ITM) or further out-of-the-money (OTM).

The put option in a long strangle, 15200PE in this case, also has a positive Gamma value. As the price of the underlying asset moves away from the strike price, whether up or down, the Gamma of the put option causes its Delta to become more sensitive to further price changes. This means that the put option's Delta will increase as the price moves either further in-the-money (ITM) or further out-of-the-money (OTM).

In a long strangle the combination of a call option with a positive Gamma and a put option having a positive Gamma creates an overall high Gamma position. This indicates that the strategy becomes more sensitive to price changes as the underlying asset's price moves away from the strike price in either direction.

Payoff *vis-à-vis* Vega

The call option in a long strangle, 15700CE in this case, has a positive Vega value. This means that any rise in implied volatility will generally increase the call option's value. Thus, higher implied volatility leads to higher option prices, potentially resulting in greater profits for the call option. Conversely, any fall in implied volatility may lower the value of the call option and any resultant gains.

The put option in a long strangle, 15200PE in this case, also has a positive Vega value. Similar to the call option, any rise in implied volatility will generally increase the value of the put option as well. Higher implied volatility therefore leads to higher option prices, potentially resulting in greater profits for the put option. Conversely, any fall in implied volatility may lower the value of the put option, and thus also lower the potential profits.

In a long strangle the combination of the call option with a positive Vega, and a put option also having a positive Vega, creates a position with a relatively high overall positive Vega. This means that any increase in implied volatility will generally benefit the overall strategy by increasing the value of both the call and put options. Conversely, any fall in implied volatility may adversely affect the gains from the strategy.

Payoff *vis-à-vis* Theta

The call option in a long strangle, 15700CE in this case, has a negative Theta value. All else being equal, this means that as time passes the value of the call option will fall. The Theta of the call option will typically be higher for options with shorter time to expiration. Time decay works against the strategy's potential profitability from the call option leg.

The put option in a long strangle, 15200PE in this case, also has a negative Theta value. Similar to the situation of the call option, as time passes the value of the put option will reduce. The Theta of the put option will also typically be higher for options with shorter time to expiration. Thus time decay works against the strategy's potential profitability from the put option leg as well.

In a long strangle the combination of a call option with negative Theta, and the put option also having a negative Theta, creates a trade position with a relatively high overall negative Theta. Thus, as time passes the strategy generally experiences time decay that can erode its potential profitability. However, the strategy's profitability finally depends on the price movement's magnitude. Traders should consider the timing of their entry into the strategy, and also the potential magnitude of price movement required to overcome time decay and generate a profit.

Summary

In this chapter we have discussed:

- How the long strangle works.

- What the payoff from this strategy could be at different levels of market expiry.
- How Greeks impact the payoff from this strategy.

Let's go ahead to our next strategy.

~

14

~

Short Strangle

THIS IS THE FOURTH OF THE NEUTRAL STRATEGIES presented in this book.

First we will look at the short strangle strategy in a concise manner. Thereafter we will consider its payoff graph and payoff table for you to visualize the various profit and loss scenarios for different levels of underlying expiry. Finally, we will consider the effect of option Greeks on a short strangle.

Short Strangle in a Nutshell

Short strangle is a strategy which you can profitably deploy when:

- Market volatility is low; and
- You think that the market will not move much in either direction till the upcoming expiry.

In such a situation you can use the short strangle with the aim of making a decent profit in a low volatile, sideways market.

The short strangle is an enhancement of the short straddle strategy. Remember, in a short straddle the trader needs to sell ATM call and put options; while in a short strangle, OTM call and put options are sold. Since OTM options are always cheaper than ATM options, short strangles are always cheaper to implement than short straddles.

Table 14.1

Short Strangle in a Nutshell

	When to Use a Short Strangle You could use a short strangle if you are neutral on the market and believe that there will not be any sizeable upward or downward price movement till the upcoming expiry.
	Trade Setup Short strangle is a two-leg strategy comprising: — Leg 1: Selling one OTM Call (CE); — Leg 2: Selling one OTM Put (PE)
	Breakeven Point There will be two points of no profits and no losses, i.e. two breakeven points in this strategy – one, if the underlying's price moves down, and another when the underlying's price moves up.
	Profit Scenarios You will make a profit if the underlying expires in between both the breakeven points.
	Loss Scenarios You will make losses if the underlying expires above the higher breakeven point, or if it expires below the lower breakeven point.
	Risk Reward Ratio ▪ Maximum risk is unlimited, and ▪ Maximum reward (₹200) is between 15,200 and 15700 levels in our hypothetical (*see* Table 14.2).
	Volatility Impact Strategy gets benefitted by decreased volatility.

(Contd . . .)

Table 14.1: **Short Strangle in a Nutshell** *(. . . contd.)*

	When to Initiate the Trade Ideally you should enter the trade 25 days, i.e. about 3-and-a-half weeks, ahead of expiry. You will get a good premium by starting early.
	When to Exit the Trade You should exit the trade: ▪ When market start trending in either direction and volatility is increasing, or ▪ The stop loss is hit, or ▪ One week before expiry, whichever event occurs first.

Let's understand this strategy in a nutshell, from start to end, for you to get a quick fix on how it works.

Payoff Diagram

Figure 14.1 depicts the payoff diagram for this strategy. As depicted by the graph, the short strangle has a limited profit potential — but unlimited risk of loss.

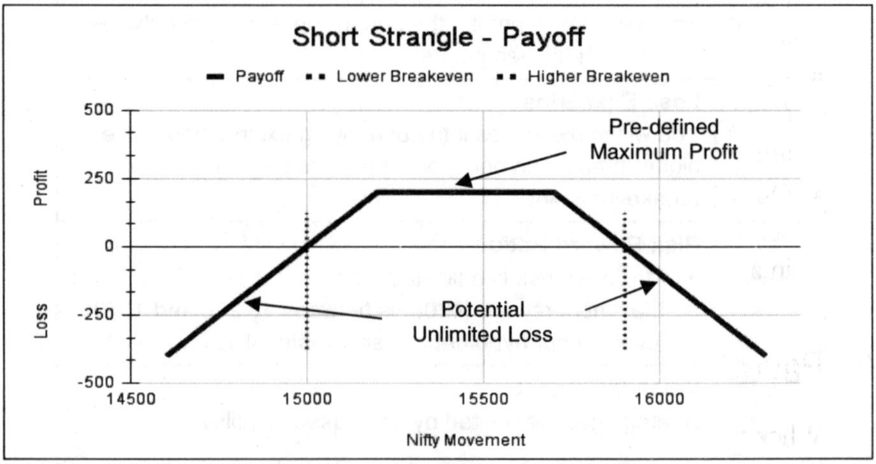

Figure 14.1: **Payoff Diagram for a Short Strangle**

Table 14.2

Particulars of Our Hypothetical Nifty Short Strangle

Particular	*Value*
Underlying	Nifty
Spot Price	15,425
Sell OTM CE	15,700
Sell OTM PE	15,200
Credit from selling call (₹)	100
Credit from selling put (₹)	100
Net Credit (₹)	100 + 100 = 200

We will consider the example of a Nifty trade since Nifty is the most widely traded derivative in India. Table 14.2 details the particulars of our hypothetical Nifty trade.

We initiate our trade with Nifty at 15425 spot levels. To deploy the two-legged short strangle strategy:

- For the first leg we sell one out-of-the-money call option (OTM 15700CE) for ₹100. That will be our credit as we are selling an option.
- For the second leg we sell one out-of-the-money put option (OTM 15200PE) for ₹100. That will also be our credit as we are again selling an option.
- Our net credit here will be ₹200 (₹100 + ₹100). Since we are selling OTM options there will always be an initial net credit in a short strangle.

Payoff Table

When the underlying Nifty moves in either direction, there will be a certain profit or loss. Table 14.3 illustrates the payoff, i.e. profit / loss, scenarios for various levels of Nifty expiry. For

ease of understanding there is a 100-point difference between each hypothetical Nifty expiry.

Table 14.3

Payoff Table for Different Levels of Nifty Expiry

Market Expiry	*Short OTM CE Strike 15700 Intrinsic Value (₹)*	*Short OTM CE Strike 15700 Payoff (₹)*	*Short OTM PE Strike 15200 Intrinsic Value (₹)*	*Short OTM PE Strike 15200 Payoff (₹)*	*Strategy Payoff (₹)*	*Comments*
14,600	0	100	600	–500	–400	Unlimited Loss Zone.
14,700	0	100	500	–400	–300	
14,800	0	100	400	–300	–200	
14,900	0	100	300	–200	–100	
15,000	0	100	200	–100	0	Lower Breakeven Point.
15,100	0	100	100	0	100	Profit Zone. Maximum Profit Capped.
15,200	0	100	0	100	200	
15,300	0	100	0	100	200	
15,400	0	100	0	100	200	
15,500	0	100	0	100	200	
15,600	0	100	0	100	200	
15,700	0	100	0	100	200	
15,800	100	0	0	100	100	
15,900	200	–100	0	100	0	Higher Breakeven Point.
16,000	300	–200	0	100	–100	Unlimited Loss Zone.
16,100	400	–300	0	100	–200	
16,200	500	–400	0	100	–300	
16,300	600	–500	0	100	–400	

From Table 14.3, you can see that the lower and higher breakeven points are exactly at 15000 and 15900, respectively.

- If Nifty expires below 15000 you will be at a loss.
- If Nifty expires above 15900 you will lose as shown in the payoff table.
- If Nifty expires at either 15000 or 15900 you will neither make a profit nor lose as this is our trade's breakeven point.
- If Nifty expires between the two breakeven points, you will make a profit through this strategy, as shown in the payoff table and the corresponding graph.

How Greeks Impact the Payoff

Having reviewed the payoff for different Nifty expiries, let's now turn to the relationship between the underlying's price movement and various option Greeks in a short strangle. We will not get into calculating the Greeks, but will focus on trying to understand how the various Greeks impact the payoff from this strategy.

Payoff *vis-à-vis* Delta

In a short strangle, the call option (15700CE in this case) has a negative Delta value. As the price of the underlying asset rises, the value of the short call option falls. The Delta of the short call option will typically be negative, and its value can approach −1 as it becomes more in-the-money (ITM).

The put option in a short strangle (15200PE in this case) has a positive Delta value. As the price of the underlying rises, the value of the short put option also increases. The Delta of the short put option will typically be positive, and its value can approach +1 as it becomes more in-the-money (ITM).

The combination of the short call option with a negative Delta, and the short put option having positive Delta, in a short strangle creates a position with an overall neutral Delta. This means that the short strangle strategy is relatively insensitive to small price movements in the underlying asset.

In fact, the short strangle strategy aims to profit from small or no price movement in the underlying asset. Income is generated from the premiums received by selling both call and put options. The risk is however potentially unlimited, both on the upside and downside due to the short call and put options.

Payoff *vis-à-vis* Gamma

The short call option in a short strangle (15700CE in this case) has a negative Gamma value. As the price of the underlying asset moves away from the strike price, whether up or down, the Gamma of the short call option causes its Delta to become more sensitive to further price changes. This means that the call option's Delta will fall as the price moves further either in-the-money (ITM) or out-of-the-money (OTM).

In a short strangle the short put option (15200PE in this case) also has a negative Gamma value. Just like in the case of the short call option, as the price of the underlying asset moves away from the strike price, whether up or down, the Gamma of the short put option causes its Delta to become more sensitive to further price changes. This means that the put option's Delta will fall as the price moves further in-the-money (ITM) or further out-of-the-money (OTM).

The combination of the short call option with a negative Gamma and the short put option also having a negative Gamma in a short strangle creates an overall high negative Gamma position. This indicates that the strategy becomes more sensitive to price changes as the underlying's price moves away from the strike price in either direction.

Payoff *vis-à-vis* Vega

In a short strangle the short call option (15700CE in this case) has a negative Vega value. This means that any rise in implied volatility will generally increase the value of the short call option, in turn, leading to higher option prices, and potentially resulting in greater losses for the short call option. Conversely, a fall in implied volatility may lower the value of the short call option.

In a short strangle the short put option (15200PE in this case) also has a negative Vega value. Similar to the case with the short call option, any rise in implied volatility will generally increase the value of the short put option. A higher implied volatility in turn leads to higher option prices, potentially resulting in greater losses for the short put option. Conversely, a fall in implied volatility may lower the value of the short put option.

The combination of the short call option with a negative Vega and the short put option also having negative Vega in a short strangle creates a trade position with a relatively high overall negative Vega. This means that any increase in implied volatility will adversely affect the overall strategy.

Payoff *vis-à-vis* Theta

In a short strangle the short call option (15700CE in this case) has positive Theta value. This means that all else being equal, the value of the short call option will fall with the passage of time. This time decay works in favour of the strategy's potential profitability from the short call option leg.

In a short strangle the short put option (15200PE in this case) also has a positive Theta value. Similar to the case with the short call option, as time passes the value of the short put option will also fall. This time decay works in favour of the strategy's potential profitability from the short put option leg.

In a short strangle the combination of a short call option with a positive Theta, and the short put option also having a positive Theta, creates a position with a relatively high overall positive Theta. This means that as time passes, the time decay can contribute to its potential profitability. **However, the strategy's profitability essentially depends on the magnitude of the underlying's price movement.** Theta has a direct impact on the short strangle strategy's profitability over time.

Summary

In this chapter we have discussed:

- How the short strangle works.
- What the payoff from this strategy would be at different levels of the underlying's expiry.
- How Greeks impact the payoff from this strategy.

Let's now go on to our next strategy.

15 ~ Iron Butterfly

THIS IS THE FIFTH IN OUR GROUP OF DELTA NEUTRAL strategies presented in this book.

First we will see iron butterfly in a concise manner. Thereafter we will consider its payoff diagram and payoff table in order to visualize the various profit and loss scenarios for different market expiries. In the end we will review the effect of option Greeks on an iron butterfly.

Iron Butterfly in a Nutshell

Iron butterfly is a strategy which you can deploy:

- When the market volatility is low:
- You expect that the market will not move much in either positive or negative direction till the upcoming expiry;
- When you want to limit your losses in case of any sudden trending move that may develop, and
- You want to make a decent profit in a low volatile, sideways market where there is no up or down trend.

Iron butterfly is a combination of the short straddle and long strangle strategies discussed earlier. The short straddle has limited profit potential if the market stays in between the two breakeven points, but runs the risk of unlimited loss if the breakeven points are breached and the market starts trending. Long strangle, on the other hand, has a limited loss possibility if the market stays in between the two breakeven points. On the other hand, it has unlimited profit potential if the breakeven point is breached due to a trending move. When we combine these two strategies, we get the iron butterfly strategy which has both limited profit potential and a limited risk of loss.

Table 15.1 encapsulates the iron butterfly strategy in a nutshell, from start to end, for you to get a quick fix on how it works.

Table 15.1

Iron Butterfly in a Nutshell

	When to Use Iron Butterfly When you are neutral on the market and think that there will not be any significant upward or downward movement till the upcoming expiry. At the same time, you want to limit your losses in case the market begins trending.
	Trade Setup Iron butterfly is a four-leg strategy comprising: — Leg 1: Selling one ATM Call (CE); — Leg 2: Selling one ATM Put (PE); — Leg 3: Buying one OTM Call (CE); — Leg 4: Buying one OTM Put (PE).
	Breakeven Point There will be two points of no profits and no losses in this strategy — one, when the underlying's price moves down, and, another, in case the underlying's price moves up.
	Profit Scenarios You will make pre-defined profits if the underlying expires in between the two breakeven points.

(Contd . . .)

Table 15.1: **Iron Butterfly in a Nutshell** *(. . . contd.)*

	Loss Scenarios You will make pre-defined losses if the underlying expires above the higher breakeven point, or if the underlying expires below the lower breakeven point.
	Risk Reward Ratio ▪ Maximum risk (₹200) is below the lower breakeven point and above the higher breakeven point in our hypothetical trade (*see* Table 15.2). ▪ Maximum reward (₹200) is at 15400 levels for our hypothetical trade (*see* Table 15.2). So, risk reward ratio will be 1:1 here.
	Volatility Impact Strategy gets benefitted by decreased volatility.
	When to Initiate the Trade Ideally, you should enter a trade 25 days, i.e. about 3-and-a-half weeks, ahead of expiry. You will get a good premium by starting early.
	When to Exit the Trade You should exit the trade: ▪ When market started trending in either direction and volatility is increasing, or ▪ The stop loss is hit, or ▪ One week before expiry, whichever event occurs first.

Payoff Diagram

Figure 15.1 is the payoff diagram for the iron butterfly strategy. As depicted by the graph, iron butterfly has both a limited profit potential and a limited loss potential.

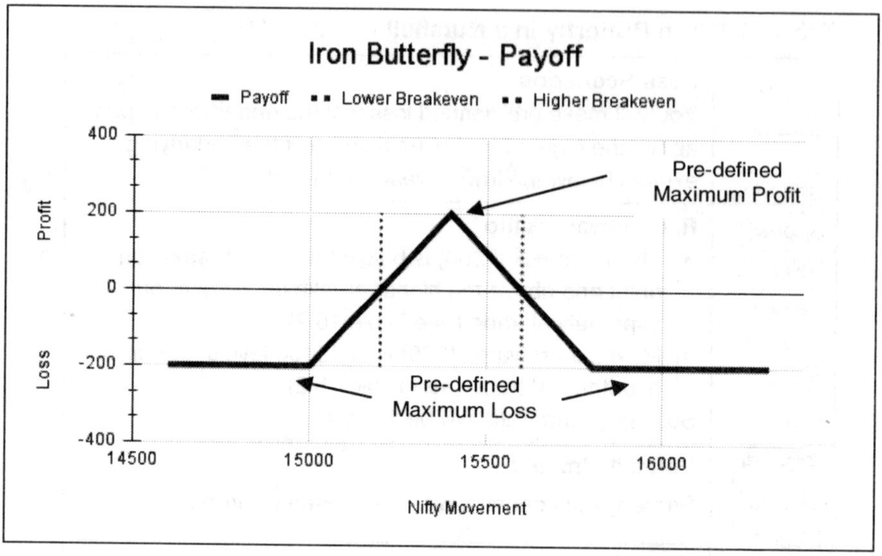

Figure 15.1: **Payoff diagram for Iron Butterfly**

We will consider the example of a Nifty trade here as Nifty is the most widely traded derivative in India. Table 15.2 highlights the particulars of our hypothetical Nifty iron butterfly trade.

We initiate our hypothetical trade with Nifty at 15,425 spot levels. To deploy the four-legged iron butterfly strategy:

- For the first leg we will sell one at-the-money call option (ATM 15400CE) for ₹125. That will be our credit as we are selling an option.
- For the second leg we will sell one at-the-money put option (ATM 15400PE) for ₹125. That will also be our credit as we are again selling an option.
- For the third leg we will buy one out-of-the-money call option (OTM 15800CE) for ₹25. That will be our debit as we are buying an option.

Table 15.2

Our Hypothetical Nifty Iron Butterfly Trade

Particular	*Value*
Underlying	Nifty
Spot Price	15,425
Sell ATM CE	15,400
Sell ATM PE	15,400
Buy OTM CE	15,800
Buy OTM PE	15,000
Credit from selling a call (₹)	125
Credit from selling a put (₹)	125
Debit from buying a call (₹)	25
Debit from buying a put (₹)	25
Net Credit (₹)	125+125–25–25 = 200

- For the fourth and final leg we will buy one out-of-the-money put option (OTM 15000CE) for ₹25. That will also be a debit as we are buying an option.
- Our net credit here will thus be ₹200 (125+125–25–25). Since you are selling ATM options and buying OTM options, there will always be an initial net credit in this strategy since ATM options are always pricier than the OTM options.

Payoff Table

When the underlying Nifty moves in either direction, there will be a certain profit or loss. Table 15.3 illustrates the payoff, i.e. profit / loss, scenarios for various levels of Nifty expiry. For ease of understanding there is a 100-point difference between each hypothetical Nifty expiry.

Table 15.3

Payoff Table for Different Levels of Nifty Expiry

Market Expiry	*Short ATM CE Strike 15400 Intrinsic Value (₹)*	*Short ATM CE Strike 15400 Payoff (₹)*	*Short ATM PE Strike 15400 Intrinsic Value (₹)*	*Short ATM PE Strike 15400 Payoff (₹)*	*Long OTM CE Strike 15800 Intrinsic Value (₹)*	*Long OTM CE Strike 15800 Payoff (₹)*	*Long OTM PE Strike 15000 Intrinsic Value (₹)*	*Long OTM PE Strike 15000 Payoff (₹)*	*Strategy Payoff (₹)*	*Comments*
14,600	0	125	800	−675	0	−25	400	375	−200	Limited Loss Zone. Maximum Loss Capped.
14,700	0	125	700	−575	0	−25	300	275	−200	
14,800	0	125	600	−475	0	−25	200	175	−200	
14,900	0	125	500	−375	0	−25	100	75	−200	
15,000	0	125	400	−275	0	−25	0	−25	−200	
15,100	0	125	300	−175	0	−25	0	−25	−100	
15,200	0	125	200	−75	0	−25	0	−25	0	Lower Break-even Point.
15,300	0	125	100	25	0	−25	0	−25	100	Profit Zone.
15,400	0	125	0	125	0	−25	0	−25	200	
15,500	100	25	0	125	0	−25	0	−25	100	
15,600	200	−75	0	125	0	−25	0	−25	0	Higher Break-even Point.
15,700	300	−175	0	125	0	−25	0	−25	−100	Limited Loss Zone. Maximum Loss Capped.
15,800	400	−275	0	125	0	−25	0	−25	−200	
15,900	500	−375	0	125	100	75	0	−25	−200	
16,000	600	−475	0	125	200	175	0	−25	−200	
16,100	700	−575	0	125	300	275	0	−25	−200	
16,200	800	−675	0	125	400	375	0	−25	−200	
16,300	900	−775	0	125	500	475	0	−25	−200	

From Table 15.3 you can see that the lower and higher breakeven points will be at 15200 and 15600, respectively.

- If Nifty expires below 15200, you will make a pre-defined loss.
- If Nifty expires above 15600 you will again make a pre-defined or limited loss as shown in Table 15.3.
- If Nifty expires at 15200, or at 15600, you will neither make a profit nor lose money as these are the two breakeven points.
- If Nifty expires in between the two breakeven points, you will make a profit through this strategy, as shown in (Table 15.3) and the corresponding graph (Figure 15.1).

How Greeks Impact the Payoff

Having reviewed the payoff table for different Nifty expiries, let's understand the relationship between the underlying's price movement and the various option Greeks for the iron condor. We will not get into calculating the Greeks, but will focus instead on trying to understand how the various Greeks impact the payoff from this strategy.

Payoff *vis-à-vis* Delta

In the iron butterfly the short call option, 15400CE in this case, has a negative Delta value. Accordingly, as the price of the underlying asset rises, the value of the short call option falls. The Delta of the short call option will typically be negative, and its value can approach −1 as it becomes more in-the-money (ITM).

The short put option in an iron butterfly, 15400PE in this case, has a positive Delta value. As the price of the underlying asset rises, the value of the short put option also increases. The Delta of the short put option will typically be positive, and its value can approach +1 as it becomes more in-the-money (ITM).

The long call option in iron butterfly (15800CE in this case) has a positive Delta value. Thus, as the price of the underlying asset rises, the value of the long call option would also increase.

The long put option in iron butterfly (15200PE in this case) has a negative Delta value. Accordingly, as the price of the underlying asset rises, the value of the long put option will fall.

The combination of a short call option with a negative Delta, a short put option having a positive Delta, a long call option with a positive Delta, and a long put option having a negative Delta in the iron butterfly creates a trade position with an overall neutral Delta. This means that the strategy is relatively insensitive to small price movements in the underlying asset.

The iron butterfly strategy aims to profit from either small or no price movement in the underlying asset. The strategy generates income from the premiums received for selling the call and put options. Both the risk and the reward are limited for this strategy.

Payoff *vis-à-vis* Gamma

The short call option (15400CE) and the short put option (15400PE) in our example of an iron butterfly trade have negative Gamma values. As the price of the underlying asset moves away from the ATM strike prices, whether up or down, the Gamma of these options causes their Deltas to become more sensitive to further price changes. Thus, Deltas of the short call and short put options will fall as the price moves either further in-the-money (ITM) or further out-of-the-money (OTM).

The long call option (15800CE) and the long put option (15200PE) in an iron butterfly have positive Gamma values. As the price of the underlying asset moves away from the OTM strike prices, whether either up or down, the Gamma of these options causes their Deltas to become more sensitive to further price changes. This means that the Deltas of the long call and the long put option will rise as the price moves further either in-the-money (ITM) or out-of-the-money (OTM).

In an iron butterfly, the combination of the short call option having a negative Gamma, the short put option also with a negative Gamma, the long call option having a positive Gamma, and the long put option having positive Gamma creates a position with an overall negative Gamma. This indicates that the strategy becomes more sensitive to price changes as the underlying asset's price moves away from both the ATM and OTM strike prices.

Payoff *vis-à-vis* Vega

The 15400CE short call option and the 15400PE short put option in an iron butterfly have negative Vega values. This means that any increase in implied volatility will generally increase the values of both short call option and the short put option resulting in potential losses from these legs. Conversely, a fall in implied volatility may decrease the value of the short options, leading to profits from these legs.

The long call option, 15800CE in this case, and the long put option (15200PE) in our iron butterfly trade both have positive Vega values. This means that any increase in implied volatility will generally increase the value of both the long call option and the long put option legs, resulting in potentially greater profits from the long options. Conversely, any reduction in implied volatility may lower the value of the long options, resulting in losses from both long call and long put options.

In an iron butterfly, the combination of the short call option with a negative Vega, the short put option with a negative

Vega, the long call option having a positive Vega, and the long put option having a positive Vega creates a trade position with an overall relatively negative Vega. This means that any increase in implied volatility will adversely affect the strategy.

Payoff *vis-à-vis* Theta

The short call option and the short put option in an iron butterfly have positive Theta values. This means that all else being equal, as time passes the values of both the short call option and the short put option will fall. The Theta of these options will typically be higher for options with shorter time to expiration. Thus, the time decay works in favour of the strategy's potential profitability from the two short options.

Both the long call option (15800CE in this case) and the long put option (15200PE in this case) have negative Theta values in an iron butterfly. This means that with the passage of time, the values of both the long call option and the long put option will fall. The Theta of these options will also typically be higher for options with shorter time to expiration. Thus time decay works against the strategy's potential profitability from the long option legs.

The combination of the short call option with positive Theta, the short put option (with positive Theta), the long call option (having a negative Theta), and the long put option (having a negative Theta) in an iron butterfly creates a trading position with an overall positive Theta. This means that as time passes, the strategy generally experiences time decay which works in favour of its potential profitability. However, the strategy's profitability depends on the price movement's magnitude.

Theta has a direct impact on the iron butterfly strategy's profitability over time. Traders should consider the timing of their entry in this strategy (as mentioned in Table 15.1) and the potential magnitude of price movement required to overcome time decay and generate a profit.

Summary

In this chapter we have discussed:

- How the iron butterfly works.
- What would the payoff from this strategy be at different market / underlying levels of expiry.
- How Greeks impact the payoff of this strategy.

Let's now go ahead to our next and final neutral strategy.

~

16

~

Iron Condor

THIS IS THE SIXTH AND FINAL STRATEGY in our group of neutral strategies.

First we will review the iron condor in a concise manner. Thereafter we will consider this strategy's payoff diagram and payoff table in order to visualize the various profit and loss scenarios for different market expiries. In the end we will review the effect of option Greeks on the iron condor.

Iron Condor in a Nutshell

Iron condor is a strategy which can be profitably deployed when:

- Market volatility is low.
- You expect that the market will not move either much higher, or much lower, till the upcoming expiry.
- Accordingly, you want to limit your losses in case of any sudden trending moves by the underlying.

In other words, you can use the iron condor strategy to make a decent profit in low volatility conditions and where the market / underlying is essentially moving sideways without any directional trend.

Table 16.1

Iron Condor in a Nutshell

	When to Use Iron Condor When you have a neutral view on the market and think that there will not be any big upward or downward market movement till the upcoming expiry. At the same time, you want to limit your losses in case the underlying does start trending.
	Trade Setup Iron condor is a four-leg strategy, comprising: — Leg 1: Selling one OTM Call (CE); — Leg 2: Selling one OTM Put (PE); — Leg 3: Buying one further OTM Call (CE); — Leg 4: Buying one further OTM Put (PE).
	Breakeven Point There will be two points of no profits and no losses, i.e. two breakeven points, in this strategy — one, if the underlying's price moves downward, and another when the underlying's price moves up.
	Profit Scenarios You will make defined profits if the underlying expires in between the two breakeven points.
	Loss Scenarios You will make defined losses if the underlying expires either above the higher breakeven point, or below the lower breakeven point.
	Risk Reward Ratio ▪ Maximum risk (₹100) is below the lower breakeven point and above the higher breakeven point for our hypothetical trade (*see* Table 16.2), and ▪ Maximum reward (₹100) is between the lower and higher breakeven points for our hypothetical trade (*see* Table 16.2). So, risk reward ratio will be 1:1 here.

(Contd . . .)

Table 16.1: **Iron Condor in a Nutshell** *(. . . contd.)*

	Volatility Impact Strategy gets benefitted by decreased volatility.
	When to Initiate the Trade Ideally you should initiate the trade 25 days, about 3-and-a-half weeks, ahead of expiry. You will get a good premium if you start early.
	When to Exit the Trade You should exit the trade: ▪ When market started trending in either direction and volatility is increasing, or ▪ The stop loss is hit, or ▪ One week before expiry, whichever event occurs first.

Iron condor is a combination of the short strangle and long strangle strategies discussed earlier. As we saw, a short strangle has a limited profit potential if the underlying stays in between the breakeven points but can lead to unlimited losses if the underlying asset begins trending and the breakeven point is breached. The long strangle, on the other hand, has a limited risk of loss if the underlying stays in between the breakeven points but has unlimited profit potential if the breakeven point is breached and the market starts trending. When we combine these two strategies, we get the iron condor strategy which has both limited profit and limited loss potential.

Iron condor is an improvement over the iron butterfly. In the case of iron butterfly, we sell ATM call and put options of the same strike — and to limit our losses, we buy OTM call and put options. In an iron condor by contrast, we sell slightly OTM call and put options, and to limit our losses we buy further OTM call and put options. Selling OTM options will always fetch lower premiums than would selling the ATM options; hence iron condor will always get you lower premiums than does an iron butterfly. However, the breakeven points in an iron condor will have a bigger spread than in the case of iron butterfly — and so the profit probability of iron condor will be higher than in the iron butterfly strategy.

Table 16.1 encapsulates the features of the iron condor in a nutshell, from start to end, for you to get a quick fix on how this strategy works.

Payoff Diagram

The payoff diagram for the iron condor strategy is plotted in Figure 16.1. As depicted by the graph, this strategy has both limited profit and limited loss potentials.

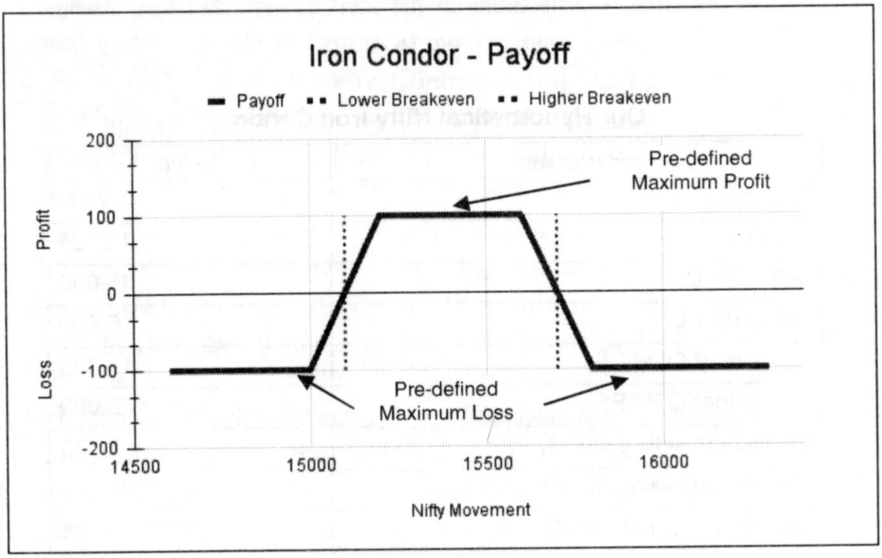

Figure 16.1: **Payoff Diagram for the Iron Condor**

We will use the example of a Nifty trade here as Nifty is the most widely traded derivative in India. Table 16.2 of lists the particulars of our hypothetical Nifty iron condor trade.

We initiate our trade with Nifty at 15425 spot levels. To deploy the four-legged iron condor strategy:

- For the first leg we will sell one out-of-the-money call option (OTM 15600CE) for ₹75. That will be our credit as we are selling an option.
- For the second leg we will sell one out-of-the-money put option (OTM 15200PE) for ₹75. That will also be our credit as we are selling an option.
- For the third leg we will buy one further out-of-the-money call option (OTM 15800CE) for ₹25. That will be our debit as we are buying an option.

Table 16.2

Our Hypothetical Nifty Iron Condor

Particular	*Value*
Underlying	Nifty
Spot Price	15,425
Sell OTM CE	15,600
Sell OTM PE	15,200
Buy further OTM CE	15,800
Buy further OTM PE	15,000
Credit from selling call (₹)	75
Credit from selling put (₹)	75
Debit from buying call (₹)	25
Debit from buying put (₹)	25
Net Credit (₹)	75 + 75 – 25 –25 = 100

- For the fourth and final leg we will buy one further out-of-the-money put option (OTM 15000CE) for ₹25. That will also be our debit as we are again buying an option.

Our net credit here will be ₹100 (75 + 75 − 25 −25). Since we are selling OTM options and buying further OTM options there will always be an initial net credit in this strategy as OTM options are always pricier than the further OTM options.

Payoff Table

When the underlying Nifty moves in either direction, there will be a certain profit or loss. Table 16.3 illustrates the payoff, i.e. profit / loss, scenarios for various levels of Nifty expiry. For ease of understanding there is a 100-point difference between each hypothetical Nifty expiry.

From Table 16.3, you can see that lower and higher breakeven points will be at 15100 and 15700, respectively.

- If Nifty expires below 15100, you will make a pre-determined loss.
- If Nifty expires above 15700 you will again make a pre-defined, or limited, loss as shown in the payoff table.
- If Nifty expires either at 15100 or at 15700 you will make neither a profit nor a loss as these are our breakeven points.
- If Nifty expires anywhere in between the two breakeven points, you will make a profit in this iron condor trade, as shown in the payoff table and the corresponding graph.

Table 16.3

Payoff Table for Different Levels of Nifty Expiry

Market Expiry	*Short OTM CE Strike 15600 Intrinsic Value (₹)*	*Short OTM CE Strike 15600 Payoff (₹)*	*Short OTM PE Strike 15200 Intrinsic Value (₹)*	*Short OTM PE Strike 15200 Payoff (₹)*	*Long Further OTM CE Strike 15800 Intrinsic Value (₹)*	*Long Further OTM CE Strike 15800 Payoff (₹)*	*Long Further OTM PE Strike 15000 Intrinsic Value (₹)*	*Long Further OTM PE Strike 15000 Payoff (₹)*	*Strategy Payoff (₹)*	*Comments*
14,600	0	75	600	−525	0	−25	400	375	−100	Limited Loss Zone. Maximum Loss Capped.
14,700	0	75	500	−425	0	−25	300	275	−100	
14,800	0	75	400	−325	0	−25	200	175	−100	
14,900	0	75	300	−225	0	−25	100	75	−100	
15,000	0	75	200	−125	0	−25	0	−25	−100	
15,100	0	75	100	−25	0	−25	0	−25	0	Lower Break-even Point.
15,200	0	75	0	75	0	−25	0	−25	100	Limited Profit Zone. Maximum Profit Capped.
15,300	0	75	0	75	0	−25	0	−25	100	
15,400	0	75	0	75	0	−25	0	−25	100	
15,500	0	75	0	75	0	−25	0	−25	100	
15,600	0	75	0	75	0	−25	0	−25	100	
15,700	100	−25	0	75	0	−25	0	−25	0	Higher Break-even Point.
15,800	200	−125	0	75	0	−25	0	−25	−100	Limited Loss Zone. Maximum Loss Capped.
15,900	300	−225	0	75	100	75	0	−25	−100	
16,000	400	−325	0	75	200	175	0	−25	−100	
16,100	500	−425	0	75	300	275	0	−25	−100	
16,200	600	−525	0	75	400	375	0	−25	−100	
16,300	700	−625	0	75	500	475	0	−25	−100	

How Greeks Impact the Payoff

Having understood the payoff for different Nifty expiries from Table 16.3, let's understand the relationship between the price movement and various option Greeks for the iron condor trade. We will not get into calculating the Greeks, but will focus instead on trying to understand how the various Greeks impact the payoff from this strategy.

Payoff *vis-à-vis* Delta

In an iron condor the short call option (15600CE in this case) has a negative Delta value. As the price of the underlying asset rises, the value of the short call option falls. The Delta of the short call option will typically be negative, and its value can approach −1 as it becomes increasingly in-the-money (ITM).

The short put option in an iron condor, 15200PE in this case, has a positive Delta value. As the price of the underlying asset rises, the value of the short put option also increases. The Delta of the short put option will typically be positive, and its value can approach +1 as it becomes more and more in-the-money (ITM).

The long call option (15800CE in this case) has a positive Delta value in an iron condor. As the price of the underlying asset rises, the value of the long call option also increases.

The long put option in an iron condor (15000PE in this case) has a negative Delta value. As the price of the underlying asset rises, the value of the long put option falls.

The combination of a short call option having negative Delta, a short put option with a positive Delta, a long call option with a positive Delta, and a long put option having negative Delta creates an overall neutral Delta position in an iron condor. This means that the iron condor strategy is relatively unaffected by small price movements in the underlying asset.

The iron condor strategy aims to profit from small or flat price movement in the underlying asset. The strategy generates income from the premiums received from selling both the call and put options, and both the risk and reward are limited for this strategy.

Payoff *vis-à-vis* Gamma

The short call option (15600CE in this case) and the short put option (15200PE in this case) in an iron condor have negative Gamma values. As the price of the underlying asset moves away from the central strike prices, whether up or down, the Gamma of these options causes their Deltas to become more sensitive to further price changes. This means that the Deltas of both short call and short put options will reduce as the price moves further in-the-money (ITM), or further out-of-the-money (OTM).

The long call option (15800CE in this case) and the long put option (15000PE in this case) in an iron condor have positive Gamma values. As the price of the underlying asset moves away from the outer strike prices, whether up or down, the Gamma of these options causes its Deltas to become more sensitive to further price changes. This means that the Deltas of both the long call and long put options will increase as the price moves either further in-the-money (ITM), or further out-of-the-money (OTM).

The combination of the short call option having a negative Gamma, the short put option with a negative Gamma, the long call option having a positive Gamma, and the long put option with a positive Gamma in an iron condor creates a position with an overall negative Gamma. This indicates that the strategy becomes more sensitive to price changes as the underlying asset's price moves away from both the OTM and further OTM strike prices.

Payoff *vis-à-vis* Vega

The short call option, and the short put option in an iron condor have negative Vega values. This means that any increase in implied volatility will generally increase the value of both short call and short put options, potentially resulting in losses from these legs. Conversely, any reduction in implied volatility may lower the value of the short options, leading to profits from these legs.

The long call option and the long put option in an iron condor have positive Vega values. This means that any rise in implied volatility will generally increase the value of both long call and long put options. Higher implied volatility leads to higher option prices, potentially resulting in greater profits for the long options. Conversely, any reduction in implied volatility may lower the value of the long options, resulting in losses from long call and long put options.

In an iron condor, the combination of the short call option with a negative Vega, the short put option having a negative Vega, the long call option with a positive Vega, and the long put option having a positive Vega creates a position with a negative overall Vega. This means that any increase in implied volatility may adversely affect the strategy.

Payoff *vis-à-vis* Theta

In an iron condor the short call option and the short put option have positive Theta values. This means that all else being equal, as time passes the value of both the short call option and the short put option will reduce. The Theta of these options will typically be higher for options with shorter time to expiration.

Thus time decay works in favour of the strategy's potential profitability from the short options.

The long call option and the long put option in an iron condor have negative Theta values. This means that the value of the long call option and the long put option will fall with the passage of time. The Theta of these options will also typically be higher for options with shorter time to expiration. This time decay works against the strategy's potential profitability from the long options.

In an iron condor the combination of a short call option with a positive Theta, a short put option with a positive Theta, a long call option having a negative Theta, and a long put option having a negative Theta creates a trade with a positive overall Theta. This means that time decay generally works in favour of its potential profitability. However, the strategy's profitability depends on the magnitude of the price movement.

Theta has a direct impact on the iron condor strategy's profitability over time. Traders should consider the timing of their entry into the strategy, as highlighted in Table 16.1, and the potential magnitude of price movement required to overcome time decay and generate a profit.

Summary

In this chapter we have discussed:

- How the iron condor works.
- What the payoffs from the strategy would be at different market expiries.
- How Greeks impact the payoff from this strategy.

Let's now turn to next section in this book which tackles hedging strategies.

Part 4
~
Hedging Strategies

— For Protecting Your Stock and Derivatives Positions Against Market Fluctuations

17

~

Synthetic Call Options

HEDGING STRATEGIES ARE TECHNIQUES used in financial markets by investors and traders to reduce or mitigate potential losses that could arise from adverse price movements. These strategies involve either taking offsetting positions *vis-à-vis* the ending holdings, or using financial instruments that can act as insurance against unfavourable price changes. Hedging strategies are commonly employed to manage risk and protect investment portfolios from market volatility, particularly by large institutional investors. Common hedging strategies include synthetic options.

Synthetic options are trading strategies that replicate the payoff and risk characteristics of normal options — but do so by using a combination of financial instruments other than options, typically stocks.

They are created by using a combination of assets to mimic the behaviour of a specific type of option, such as a call option or a put option, without directly using the option contract itself.

The goal of using synthetic options is often to achieve a similar market position as is achieved by holding an actual option, but with potential cost savings. The following are two common types of synthetic options:

- Synthetic call options; and
- Synthetic put options.

In this chapter we will discuss synthetic call options in detail.

A synthetic call option is created by combining a long position in the underlying asset, say a stock, with a long position in An ATM put option. This combination aims to replicate the risk and reward profile of holding a call option. Thus:

- If the stock's price rises, the value of the long stock position will also increase, offsetting any loss in the long put position.
- Conversely, if the stock's price falls, the value of the long put position will increase, offsetting the loss in the long stock position.
- The payoff of a synthetic call option mirrors that of an actual call option, where potential profits are unlimited, but losses are limited to the initial option premium paid for buying the ATM put option.

Synthetic Call Option in a Nutshell

Table 17.1 encapsulates this strategy in a nutshell, from start to end, in order to get a quick fix on a synthetic call option and how a synthetic call option works.

Table 17.1

Synthetic Call Options in a Nutshell

	When to Use a Synthetic Call Option When you are holding a stock in the cash market, say, for example, Reliance, and expect to make profits if its price goes up. Yet, you want to limit your losses if its price were to go down instead in the near term.

(Contd . .)

Table 17.1: **Synthetic Call Options in a Nutshell** *(. . . contd.)*

Trade Setup Synthetic call option is a two-leg strategy comprising: — Leg 1: The stock you are holding; — Leg 2: Buying one ATM Put (PE) of the same stock.
Breakeven Point The point of no profits and no losses will be the stock's price, plus the premium paid for the ATM put option.
Profit Scenarios You will make profits if the stock expires above the breakeven point.
Loss Scenarios You will make losses equal to the premium paid if the stock expires at, or below, the breakeven point.
Risk Reward Ratio ▪ Maximum risk (₹50) is below the breakeven point for our hypothetical trade (*see* Table 17.2), and ▪ Maximum reward is unlimited once the stock starts to move up.
Volatility Impact Strategy gets benefitted by increased volatility.
When to Initiate the Trade You should be holding the underlying stock either in the cash market or as futures. The trade should be initiated at least two weeks before expiry.
When to Exit the Trade This is basically hedging strategy to protect long positions or investments. You may continue to hold Futures or stocks position if prices go down, as losses will be covered by ATM PE.

Payoff Diagram

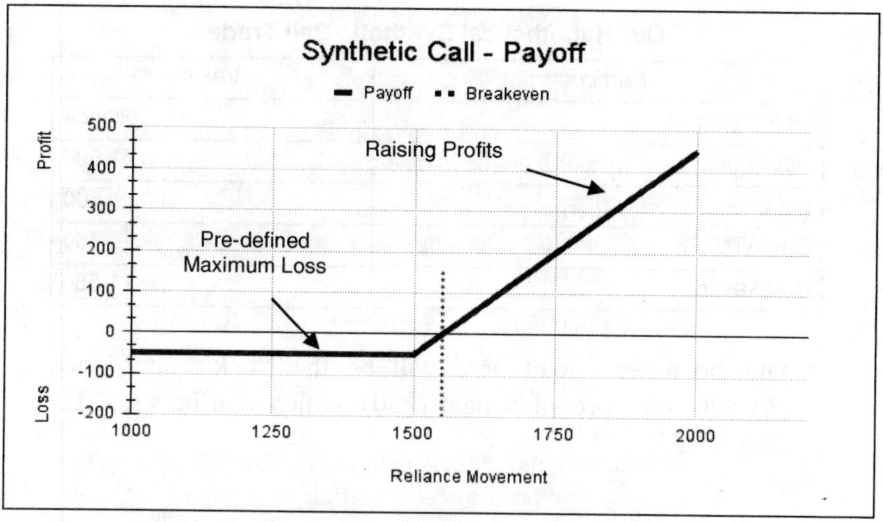

Figure 17.1: **Payoff Diagram for the Synthetic Call**

The payoff diagram for this strategy has been plotted in Figure 17.1. As depicted by the graph, a synthetic call option has unlimited potential for profit but the risk of loss is capped at the premium paid for buying the ATM put option.

We will take the example of a trade in Reliance Industries Ltd as it is one of the most traded stocks in India.

Table 17.2 lists the particulars of our hypothetical synthetic call trade.

Let's say we initiate our trade with Reliance at ₹1,500 in the cash market. To deploy this two-legged strategy:

- For the first leg we would buy and hold the stock (500 quantity), Reliance in this case.
- For the second leg we will buy one at-the-money put option (ATM 1500PE) for ₹50. That will be our debit as we are buying options.

Table 17.2

Our Hypothetical Synthetic Call Trade

Particular	*Value*
Underlying	Reliance
Spot Price	₹1,500
Lot Size	500
Buy ATM PE	₹50
Breakeven	₹1,550

- Our breakeven point here will be the stock's spot price (₹1,500) plus premium paid (₹50), which will be ₹1,500 + 50 = ₹1,550.

Payoff Table

Let's now consider the payoff table to better understand how a synthetic call works. If Reliance moves in either direction, there will be a certain profit or loss — and how much it will be at various levels of expiry can be understood from the payoff table (Table 17.3).

For ease of understanding there is a 100-point difference between the various hypothetical expiries of Reliance.

From Table 17.3, you can see that you will start to make money if the Reliance share moves above its breakeven point, which is ₹1,550. If Reliance is below its breakeven point at the time of option expiry, you will lose the premium you paid to buy the ATM PE of Reliance. In fact, that is the maximum you will lose in this strategy. Your Reliance holding will become immune to any further downward price movement because of the ATM PE option, as shown in payoff table and graph.

Table 17.3

Payoff Table for Different Levels of Reliance Expiry

Reliance Expiry	*Stock Payoff (₹)*	*Long Put Strike Intrinsic Value (₹)*	*Long Put Strike Payoff (per lot) (₹)*	*Strategy Payoff (₹)*	*Comments*
1,000	–500	500	450	-50	Capped Loss Zone.
1,100	–400	400	350	-50	
1,200	–300	300	250	-50	
1,300	–200	200	150	-50	
1,400	–100	100	50	-50	
1,500	0	0	–50	-50	
1,550	50	0	–50	0	Breakeven Zone.
1,600	100	0	–50	50	Rising Profit Zone.
1,700	200	0	–50	150	
1,800	300	0	–50	250	
1,900	400	0	–50	350	
2,000	500	0	–50	450	

You can consider the synthetic call strategy as your insurance for the underlying stock. This strategy can be deployed for any stock in which derivative trading is allowed in NSE and can be used to offset possible short term losses which might be caused due to any unexpected downtrend in the underlying.

How Greeks Impact the Payoff

Having grasped the payoff scenarios for different Nifty expiries (Table 17.3), let's understand the relationship between the stock's price movement and various option Greeks for the synthetic call strategy. We will not get into calculating the various Greeks, but will focus instead on understanding how the various Greeks impact the payoff from this strategy.

Payoff *vis-à-vis* Delta

In a synthetic call strategy, you hold a long stock position. The Delta of a long stock position is +1, meaning that for every ₹1 increase in the stock's price, the position gains ₹1. Therefore, the Delta of the long stock position contributes positively to the overall Delta of a synthetic call.

You also hold a long put option in a synthetic call strategy. The Delta of a long put option is negative and typically ranges between −1 and 0, depending on the option's strike price and its proximity to the prevailing stock price. As the stock price rises, the value of the short put falls, resulting in a decrease in the option's negative Delta.

The overall Delta of a synthetic call strategy is the sum of the Deltas of its individual components — the long stock position and the long put option. Given that the Delta of the long stock position is +1 and the Delta of the short put option is negative, the Delta's net effect is positive. This means that the strategy's Delta will be somewhere between 0 and +1, making it a bullish strategy.

Payoff *vis-à-vis* Gamma

The long stock position in a synthetic call strategy has a Gamma of 0. This means that the Gamma of the long stock position remains neutral, whatever be the changes in the stock's price.

The long put option in a synthetic call strategy has a positive Gamma value. This means that as the price of the underlying asset moves away from the strike price, whether up or down, the Gamma of the put option causes its Delta to become more sensitive to any further price changes. This behaviour of the long put's Delta changing in response to the underlying's price movement contributes positively to the strategy's overall Gamma.

Given that the long stock position's Gamma is neutral and the long put option's Gamma is positive, the overall Gamma of the synthetic call strategy will be positive. Thus the strategy's Gamma would increase when the stock's price moves away from its current price, making the strategy more sensitive to larger price movements.

Payoff *vis-à-vis* Vega

The long stock position in a synthetic call strategy has a Vega of 0. This means that changes in implied volatility do not directly affect the value of the long stock position. The Vega of the long stock position remains neutral *vis-à-vis* changes in implied volatility.

The long put option in a synthetic call strategy has a positive Vega value. This means that any increase in implied volatility will generally increase the value of the long put option. Conversely, a reduction in implied volatility may lead to a fall in the long put option's value.

Given that the long stock's Vega is neutral and the long put option's Vega is positive, the overall position Vega for a synthetic call strategy will be positive. This indicates that any increase in implied volatility will generally positively impact the overall value of the strategy, while a fall in implied volatility may have a negative impact.

Payoff *vis-à-vis* Theta

The long stock position in a synthetic call strategy has a Theta of 0. This means that time decay does not directly affect the value of the long stock position. The Theta of the long stock position remains neutral with changes in time to expiry.

The long put option in a synthetic call strategy has a negative Theta value. This means that as time passes, the value of the long put option will fall. The Theta of the long put option will typically be higher for options with longer time to expiration. This time decay works against the strategy's potential profitability from the long put option.

Given that the long stock's Theta is neutral and the long put option's Theta is negative, the overall Theta of the synthetic call position will be negative. This indicates that as time passes, it can erode the potential profitability. However, the strategy's profitability depends on the magnitude of the underlying price movement. Traders should consider the timing of their entry into the strategy, and the potential magnitude of price movement required to overcome time decay and generate a profit.

Summary

In this chapter we have discussed:

- How a synthetic call works.
- What will be the payoff from this strategy at different stock expiries.
- How Greeks impact the payoff from this strategy.

Let's go ahead to our next and final strategy of this book.

18

~

Synthetic Put Options

THIS IS THE SECOND, AND FINAL, HEDGING STRATEGY covered in this book. The synthetic put option strategy is conceptually similar to the synthetic call option strategy but its implementation is exactly the reverse.

A synthetic put option is created by combining a short position in the underlying asset, namely a stock futures, with a long position in a call option. This combination aims to replicate the risk and reward profile of holding a put option. If the stock's price rises, the value of the long call option will increase, offsetting the loss in the short futures position. The payoff of a synthetic put option mirrors that of an actual put option, where potential profits are significant if the stock's price falls, while losses are limited to the initial option premium paid for buying the ATM call option.

Please note that multi-day shorting of stocks in spot market is not allowed in NSE. Accordingly, in order to implement this strategy we need to short the futures contract of the stock.

Synthetic Put Option in a Nutshell

Table 18.1 encapsulates how the synthetic put option strategy works in a nutshell, from start to end.

Table 18.1

Synthetic Put Option in a Nutshell

Synthetic Put Option in a Nutshell
When to Use a Synthetic Put Option When you are short on some stock futures in the derivatives market, say, for example Reliance futures, in order to make profits as you expect the price to go down. At the same time, you also want to limit your losses if the stock's price were to go up in the near term.
Trade Setup Synthetic put option is a two-leg strategy comprising: — Leg 1: Shorting a stock futures; — Leg 2: Buying one ATM Call (CE) of same stock.
Breakeven Point The point of no profits and no losses will be the stock futures price *minus* the premium paid for buying the ATM call option.
Profit Scenarios You will make profits if the stock expires below the breakeven point.
Loss Scenarios You will make losses equal to the premium paid if the stock expires at or above the breakeven point.
Risk Reward Ratio ▪ Maximum risk (₹50) is above the breakeven point for our hypothetical trade (*see* Table 18.2), and ▪ Maximum reward is unlimited once the stock's future starts to move below the breakeven point.
Volatility Impact Strategy gets benefitted by increased volatility.

(Contd . . .)

Table 18.1: **Synthetic Put Option in a Nutshell** *(. . . contd.)*

25 DEC	**When to Initiate the Trade** You should be shorting the underlying stock's futures in derivative market. Trade should be initiated at least two weeks before expiry.
	When to Exit the Trade This is basically hedging strategy to protect short positions. You may continue to short Futures position if prices go up, as losses will be covered by ATM CE.

Payoff Diagram

The payoff diagram for the synthetic put option strategy is depicted in Figure 18.1. As shown by the graph, this strategy has unlimited profit potential but the risk or loss is limited, capped to the premium paid for buying the ATM CE option.

We will take the example of a hypothetical trade in Reliance Industries Ltd as this company's stock is one of the most traded equities in India.

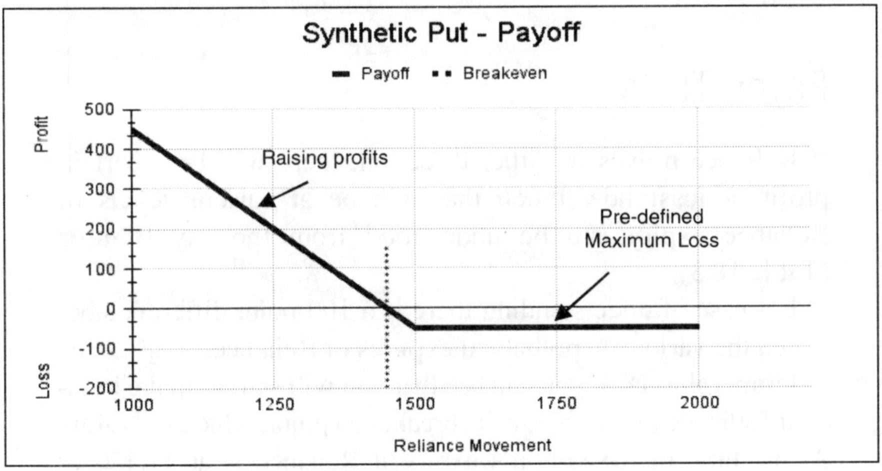

Figure 18.1: **Payoff Diagram for a Synthetic Put**

Table 18.2

Particulars of Our Hypothetical Synthetic Put Trade

Particular	*Value*
Underlying	Reliance
Spot Price	₹1,500
Lot Size	500
Buy ATM CE	₹50
Breakeven	₹1,450

Table 18.2 lists the particulars of our hypothetical synthetic put trade.

We initiate our hypothetical trade with Reliance trading at ₹1,500 in the cash market. To deploy this two-legged strategy, for the first leg we would short stock futures, Reliance in this case. For the second leg we will buy one at-the-money call option (ATM 1500CE) for ₹50. That will be our debit as we are buying an option. Our breakeven point here will be the stock spot price (₹1,500) *minus* the premium paid (₹50) which will be ₹1,450.

Payoff Table

If Reliance moves in either direction, there will be a certain profit or loss; how much that will be at various levels of Reliance expiry can be understood from the payoff table (Table 18.3).

For ease of understanding there is a 100-point difference between the various hypothetical expiries of Reliance.

From Table 18.3, you can see that you will start to make money if Reliance moves below its breakeven point, which is ₹1,450. At the time of the option's expiry if Reliance is at ₹1,450 or

Table 18.3

Payoff Table for Different Levels of Reliance Expiry

Reliance Expiry	*Stock Payoff (₹)*	*Long Call Strike Intrinsic Value (₹)*	*Long Call Strike Payoff (₹)*	*Strategy Payoff (₹)*	*Comments*
1,000	500	0	-50	450	Rising Profit Zone.
1,100	400	0	-50	350	
1,200	300	0	-50	250	
1,300	200	0	-50	150	
1,400	100	0	-50	50	
1,450	50		-50	0	Breakeven Zone.
1,500	0	0	-50	-50	Capped Loss Zone.
1,600	–100	100	50	-50	
1,700	–200	200	150	-50	
1,800	–300	300	250	-50	
1,900	–400	400	350	-50	
1,000	–500	500	450	-50	

higher, you will lose the premium you paid to buy a Reliance ATM CE. And that will be the maximum you can lose in this strategy. The underlying instrument (Reliance futures) will become immune to any further upward price movement because of the ATM CE option, as shown in the payoff table and graph.

Consider the synthetic put strategy as your insurance for shorted stock futures. This strategy can be used to offset any losses while shorting stock futures which may arise due to any unexpected uptrend in the market.

How Greeks Impact the Payoff

Having reviewed the payoff table for different Nifty expiries (Table 18.3), let's understand the relationship between the price movement and various option Greeks for the synthetic put strategy. We will not get into calculating the Greeks, but will focus instead on trying to understand how the various Greeks impact the payoff from this strategy.

Payoff *vis-à-vis* Delta

The short futures position in a synthetic put strategy has a negative Delta value. If the underlying asset's price falls, the value of the short futures position rises, benefiting the strategy. The Delta of a short futures position is typically around −1, indicating that for every ₹1 fall in the stock's price, the position gains ₹1. The negative Delta of the short futures position contributes negatively to the overall Delta of the synthetic put.

The long call option in a synthetic put strategy has a positive Delta value. As the price of the underlying asset rises, the value of the long call option also increases. The Delta of a long call option is typically between +1 and 0, depending on the option's strike price and proximity to the current stock price. The positive Delta of the long call option contributes positively to the overall Delta of a synthetic put.

The combination of a negative Delta from the short futures leg, and the positive Delta from the long call option leg, creates an overall position Delta that is typically negative. This indicates that the strategy's payoff is bearish; it benefits from downward price movements in the underlying asset. The negative Delta suggests that the strategy's value will increase as the underlying asset's price falls.

Payoff *vis-à-vis* Gamma

The short futures position in a synthetic put strategy has a Gamma of 0. This means that the Gamma of the short futures position remains neutral in the context of changes in the stock price.

The long call option in a synthetic put strategy has a positive Gamma value. This means that as the price of the underlying asset moves away from the strike price, whether up or down, the Gamma of the put option causes its Delta to become more sensitive to further price changes. This behaviour of the long call's Delta changing in response to price movements contributes positively to the strategy's overall Gamma.

Given that the Gamma of the short futures position is neutral, and the long call option's Gamma is positive, the overall Gamma of the synthetic put strategy will be positive. This indicates that the strategy's Gamma increases as the stock's price moves away from the current price, making the strategy more sensitive to larger price movements.

Payoff *vis-à-vis* Vega

The short futures position in a synthetic put strategy has a Vega of 0. This means that changes in implied volatility do not directly affect the value of the short futures position. The Vega of the short futures position remains neutral in the context of changes in implied volatility.

The long call option in a synthetic put strategy has a positive Vega value. This means that any increase in implied volatility will generally increase the value of the long call option, potentially benefiting the strategy. Conversely, any reduction in implied volatility may lead to a fall in the value of the long call option, potentially resulting in losses for the strategy.

Given that the Vega of the short futures position is neutral, and the long call option's Vega is positive, the overall position Vega of the synthetic put strategy will be positive. This indicates that any increase in implied volatility will generally impact the overall value of the strategy positively, while a reduction in implied volatility may have a negative impact.

Payoff *vis-à-vis* Theta

The short futures position in a synthetic put strategy has a Theta of 0. This means that changes in time decay (Theta) do not directly affect the value of the short futures position. The Theta of the short futures position remains neutral in the context of changes in time.

The long call option in a synthetic put strategy has a negative Theta value. This means that as time passes, the value of the long call option will fall. The Theta of the long call option will typically be higher for options with shorter time to expiry. This time decay works against the strategy's potential profitability from the long call option leg.

Given that the Theta of the short futures position is neutral, and the long call option's Theta is negative, the overall position Theta of the synthetic put strategy will be negative. This indicates that as time passes, the potential profitability is generally eroded by time decay. As time progresses, the value of the long call option falls due to negative Theta. Traders should carefully consider the timing of their entry into the strategy as well as the potential magnitude of price movement required to overcome time decay and generate a profit.

Summary

In this chapter we have discussed:

- How a synthetic put works.
- What the payoff from this strategy would be at different expiries of the underlying stock.
- How Greeks impact the payoff from this strategy.

Part 5
~
Trading Options

19

~

Key Requirements for Trading Options

TRADING OPTIONS IN REAL LIFE requires careful preparation and a thorough understanding of the derivatives market. You need to be comfortable, both financially and psychologically, before you plunge into options trading. In this chapter we will look at those aspects which will help you transit from paper trading to real trading in the market.

We now discuss some key steps and important factors to be handled in order to trade options.

Trading Account

You need to open a brokerage or trading account with a reputable trading platform. You must make sure that the brokerage account you choose provides access to derivative markets and also has a user-friendly trading platform. In India, when anyone opens a trading account, derivatives and commodity trading options are disabled by default. To be able to trade options, you need to get the derivative trading option enabled. Typically it's free of cost but please do check if enabling the derivatives option entails any charges.

In India, there are two types of brokers with whom you can open your trading account — traditional brokers and discount brokers.

Traditional, or full-service brokers as they are also known, may provide personalized advice to their clients and may also have robust trading platforms, but they charge relatively higher brokerage fees from their clients.

Discount brokers, as the name suggests, charge a much lower brokerage from their client — for instance, a flat fee per trade instead of a percentage charge — but you will not get any investment guidance or any one-to-one advisory service.

Educate Yourself

Before you start trading options, it's essential to educate yourself about how options and their dynamics work. You should understand the terminology, strategies, and risks involved. There are numerous books, online courses, and tutorials available to help you learn this. For beginners in particular, I would like to suggest that you go through my earlier book, *Making Money by Selling Options — Simplified**. The book has a detailed explanation of everything that is required to begin your options trading journey.

Psychological Preparedness

Emotions play a significant role in day-to-day trading. So it's important to be well prepared for the psychological challenges that accompany trading options, such as dealing with losses,

---

* *Making Money by Selling Options — Simplified*, published by Vision books (www.visionbooksindia.com)

and avoiding impulsive decisions driven by fear or greed. You need to be crystal clear about what you want to achieve from your trading. The market is limitless, both in terms of profit and loss. You need to decide what your boundaries and limits are, be it *vis-à-vis* profit or loss, and rules to get out of a trade when your objectives have been met, etc.

No book in this world can teach you self-control; this you need to learn and practice on your own. Without hedging, options are a very dangerous instrument. One wrong trade and your entire capital can vanish. But if you have either a proper stop-loss, or a defined risk in place, you will be saved from grievous loss most of the time. The more time you spend in the market, better prepared from a psychological standpoint you will grow.

Risk Management Plan

Developing a risk management plan is crucial for every trader. You need to define what percentage of your capital you are willing to risk on each trade, and you should set a stop-loss based on that to actually limit potential losses. For every trade, there should be a defined risk-reward ratio. This is a ratio of how much capital we are willing to risk for a certain reward. Suppose, you are expecting to collect a premium of ₹10,000 in an options trade, and the maximum risk is ₹15,000, then the risk-reward ratio will be 1.5:1. There is no ideal risk-reward ratio. This ratio will vary from trader to trader, and the unique trading style of the trader concerned. For example, if a trader is convinced that the trade will go in his favour, he might be willing to take more risk in terms of capital, increasing his risk-reward ratio.

You might have heard that options can give you potentially unlimited profit — and also unlimited loss. In real life, you will not wait for your profits to become "unlimited"; nor will you wait for your losses to go on ballooning beyond a limit.

Chances are you will close the trade well before that. If you are selling options using a hedged multi-leg strategy then your risk is well-defined. If you are trading using a naked strategy, you need to put a fresh stop loss in your trading terminal every day, since stop losses have only a one-day validity.

Trading Strategy

You need to decide on an options trading strategy that suits your goals and risk tolerance. This book provides you sound, concise knowledge on various important and popular option trading strategies. Please read and re-read these strategies carefully to make sure that you understand all their nuances and implement them as per the prevailing market conditions, or your expectation of the price movement ahead. You also need to keep a watch on your risk-reward ratio and exit a trade as soon as your target is met, or your stop-loss is hit.

Capital

You will need a minimum capital of close to ₹1 lakh in order to trade options. Earlier, it used to be higher. Then in June 2020 SEBI announced reduced margin requirements for trading options with hedged positions, namely option trades where your losses are pre-defined.

For example, in an Iron Condor strategy, explained in earlier chapters, to get the margin benefits, first we will buy the options and then we will sell the option. Today, on 2nd January 2025, Nifty is at around 24,200 levels. To initiate Iron Condor for 23rd January 2025 weekly expiry, we will;

- Buy 23,800 PE
- Sell 24,000 PE

- Sell 24,400 CE
- Buy 24,600 CE

If we buy PE and CE options first, our margin requirement will be much less while selling PE and CE to construct the Icon Condor. Below screenshot is from UpStox margin calculator (https://upstox.com/calculator/span-calculator/) which shows only 78k as final margin for above mentioned trade setup:

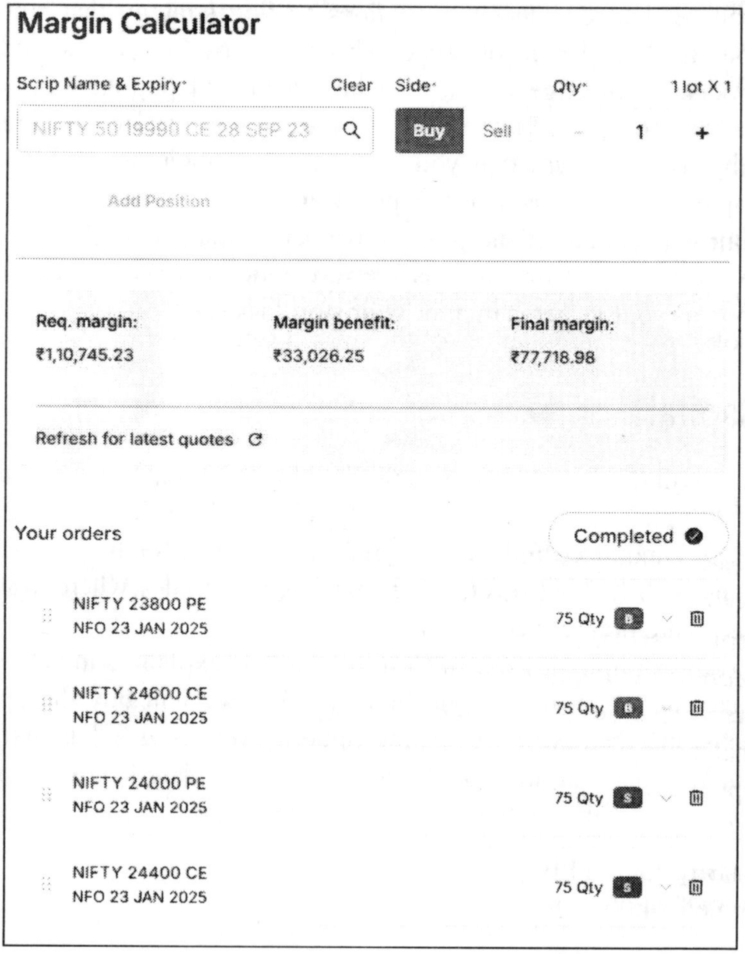

Options can be leveraged, meaning you can control a larger position with a smaller amount of capital, but this also increases risk that you need to be alert to — and to take care of.

Entering a Trade

When you enter into a trade, you need to look for certain indicators which should tell you if things are favourable for initiating a new trade setup. All of the below mentioned indicators have been explained in detail in my earlier book.*

Let's consider see these one by one. For simplicity, we have assumed that trader is initiating an iron condor trade setup.

Values of Option Greeks

When you try to trade any setup including Iron Condor, first look for the Greek values of the overall setup. You can find live Greek values on websites, like https://web.sensibull.com/ and https://opstra.definedge.com/.

Selecting Strikes

Trade should be initiated at 1SD (1-Standard Deviation) on both CE and PE sides. Calculating standard deviation is a big topic and it has been explained in my earlier book, *Making Money by Selling Options — Simplified.* I would request readers to go through the topic of calculating standard deviation in that book, if they want to pursue 1SD approach of selecting option strikes.

---

* *Making Money by Selling Options — Simplified*, published by Vision books (www.visionbooksindia.com)

Initiating the Trade

If you are selling options, you should enter the trade only at 3:00 PM. The reason for doing so is that Theta will decay overnight, and your position will start in profits the next morning. When you initiate your trade at 3:00 PM, there will be just 30 minutes of trading time remaining for the day which will limit the impact on your trade.

On the other hand, if you are an options buyer you should avoid buying options at the end of the trading day because Theta works against the long positions.

Check PCR (Put-to-Call Ratio)

You must check PCR before entering a trade. PCR value will give you a hint about the overall market's view of the upcoming market movement, and you can be prepared for that in advance:

PCR > 130 = Overbought;
PCR < 60 = Oversold;
PCR ~ 90 = Bullish;
PCR 100 = Neutral.

You can find PCR values on various websites, like https://web.sensibull.com/ and https://opstra.definedge.com/

Check Bollinger Bands Every Day

Once you have initiated your trade you should watch the Bollinger Bands on a daily basis, preferably on the daily chart. Bollinger Bands is a technical indicator, based on standard deviation, which indicates how the market may move in the upcoming trading sessions. It is a momentum indicator plotted using SMA (simple moving average), along with its standard deviation values marking the upper and lower boundaries to suggest whether the price may be too high or too low.

Watch Max OI (Open Interest)

You should watch Max OI of CE and PE on a daily basis. Max OI will tell you about any shift in the market's sentiment, and where or in which direction the market can go in the upcoming days.

Watch Max Pain

You should also keep an eye on Max Pain on a daily basis. This can give you a hint where the market could be in the last week of the option's expiry, and you can adjust your trade position accordingly.

Now a brief word about max pain. There are two types of options traders — option buyers and option sellers. Max pain theory says that options sellers are mostly big institutions, such as investment banks, mortgage companies, etc since they have big money to work with, and since their stakes are huge, they may even manipulate the market's direction to favour their existing trade positions. This theory also holds that a majority of option buyers lose money on expiry day. Accordingly, close to the expiry the market moves in the direction which would cause maximum losses for option buyers and, in-turn, maximum profits for option sellers. Max pain value indicates levels at which the market may expire in the current expiry.

Suppose a stock XYZ is trading in the cash market at ₹50 and the max pain for that stock's options is ₹52. If most options contracts expire at ₹52 or below, option writers (sellers) would experience the least financial pain because those options would expire worthless.

Similarly, consider that the Nifty index is trading at 20,000 and the max pain for Nifty might be at 19,500. If a large number of options expire at or below 19,500, it minimizes the pain for option writers.

Max pain is a concept used by some traders and analysts to gauge potential market movements based on where options are concentrated. While max pain can provide insights on the future price movement of the underlying asset, it should not be used as a certain predictor of price movement.

Watch India VIX

Keep an eye on the India VIX indicator. VIX moves inversely to Nifty's movement. If Nifty goes down, VIX moves up, and *vice-versa*. Basically, VIX points to volatility in the upcoming days. For delta neutral option positions, any increase in volatility is bad; for directional trades, on the other hand, it can be beneficial.

Start Small

If you're new to options trading, consider starting with a small amount of trading capital, and increase it gradually as you gain experience and confidence. To start with a new trader should trade only one lot. Only after a few months should you increase the number of lots you trade. Increasing your trade position size gradually will not only give you confidence in your trading skills but it will also help you overcome your emotional and psychological barriers in options trading.

Taxation

In India, options trading attracts short term capital gain tax. Please ensure that you comply with all the relevant tax laws and file your income tax returns on time. Almost all trading platforms provide various reports on profits / losses and capital gains. You need to download those reports and share them with your tax consultant. You can take help of online portals like https://cleartax.in/ as well. If you want to file your tax on the Income Tax website directly, you can follow instructions provided on https://incometaxindia.gov.in/.

You Need to Go On Learning

The options market is very complex and dynamic. You need to stay informed about market changes, new strategies, and developments in the financial industry. You need to continuously improve your knowledge and adapt your strategies accordingly.

Please remember that options trading involves a significant level of risk, and you can lose more than your initial investment. We cannot emphasize enough that it is very crucial to approach options trading with caution, proper research, and a disciplined approach.

How to Execute and Monitor Your Orders

To start with, I would recommend using either https://web.sensibull.com/ or https://opstra.definedge.com/. These platforms provide detailed strategy builders with real time implied volatility (IV), Greek values, and profit and loss scenarios on different market expiries. These platforms are not broker platforms but are meant only for analysis purposes. In the case of Sensibull, you can link your trading account (like ICICIDirect or Zerodha) and you can trade directly from Sensibull. Orders will then get executed from your trading account and you can monitor your live positions in Sensibull. In Opstra, while you can't link your trading account, but you can construct your strategy, execute that strategy in your trading account and monitor profit / loss scenario. Thus, in Sensibull you can access your trading account but in Opstra your trading account will not be linked.

Let's see what these platforms have to offer to both novice and experienced traders.

Sensibull (https://web.sensibull.com/)

Sensibull is an online platform designed to assist options traders make informed decisions. It offers a range of tools and features tailored to meet the requirements of both novice and experienced traders in the complex world of options trading. Key components of Sensibull include:

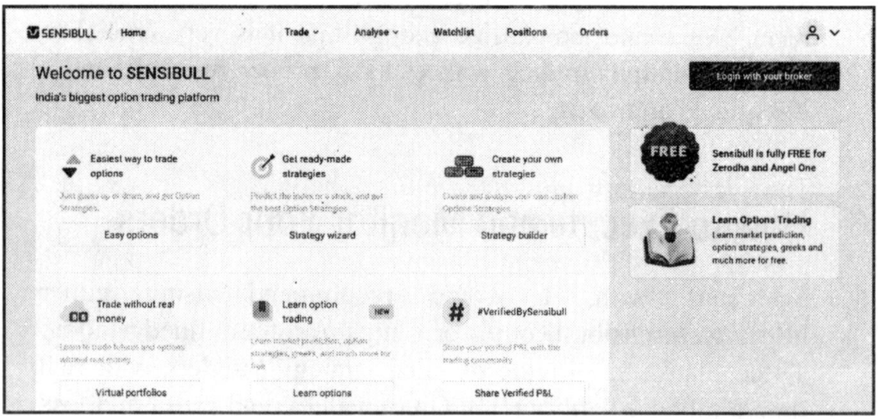

Option Chain Analysis

Sensibull provides an advanced option chain analysis tool that enables traders to quickly assess options data, including Greeks, implied volatility, and other essential metrics. This aids in understanding the potential risk and reward related to different option trading strategies.

Strategy Builder

Users can build and visualize various options trading strategies using Sensibull's user-friendly strategy builder. This feature allows traders to create, back test, and optimize strategies to meet their specific goals and risk tolerances.

Educational Resources

Sensibull offers a variety of educational materials and options trading courses. These resources cover topics ranging from the basics of options trading to advanced strategies, helping traders enhance their knowledge and skills.

Risk Management Tools

Sensibull equips traders with risk management tools to help you set stop-loss orders, track portfolio performance, and manage risk effectively.

Market Insights

The platform provides real-time market insights, news, and analysis, keeping traders informed of market developments that may impact their trading decisions.

Broker Integration

Sensibull can integrate with select brokerage platforms, thus streamlining the execution of options trades for its users.

Option Scanners

Sensibull's option scanners help users identify potential trading opportunities based on various criteria and filters which you may like to use.

Diverse Option Strategies

Sensibull offers a wide range of option strategies suitable for different market scenarios and trader objectives.

Opstra by Definedge (https://opstra.definedge.com/)

Opstra, developed by Definedge, is a specialized options analysis and strategy creation platform. It focuses on providing advanced analytics and tools for options traders. Key features of Opstra include:

1. **Advanced Analytics:** Opstra offers sophisticated options analytics, including volatility skew analysis, implied volatility (IV) rank, and more, helping traders gain insights into market conditions.

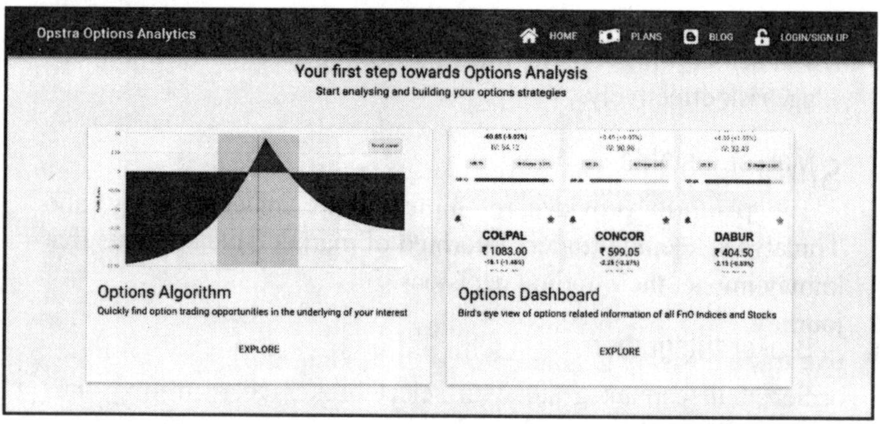

2. **Strategy Backtesting:** Traders can backtest their option strategies to assess their historical performance under various market conditions.
3. **Strategy Builder:** Opstra enables users to create and visualize complex option strategies with ease, allowing for strategy customization and optimization.
4. **Risk Management:** The platform provides tools for setting risk parameters and managing options position effectively.
5. **Historical Data:** Users can access historical options data to enhance their analysis and decision-making.
6. **Scanners and Screeners:** Opstra offers scanners and screeners to identify potential options trading opportunities based on specific criteria.
7. **Educational Resources:** The platform may offer educational content and resources to help traders enhance their options trading knowledge and skills.

Both Sensibull and Opstra cater to options traders who are seeking tools and insights to improve their trading strategies. You should visit these websites for the most up-to-date information, features, and pricing details. Of course, it's essential to have a solid understanding of options trading and the associated risks before using these platforms for actual trading.

Summary

This chapter would, hopefully, have provided you sufficient knowledge and a roadmap to embark on your options trading journey. Even if you have a trading account active with derivative trading option enabled, I urge you to paper trade first. Record all your trades on paper as if you were actually executing them in the market. Apply option strategies mentioned in the book and once you close the position on paper, you need to check how much profits or losses you have incurred. Paper trading can be a very effective method to boost your confidence without risking your capital. Alternatively, you can use the strategy builder and virtual trading feature of Sensibull or Opstra. Both the platforms provide these features where you can execute dummy trades without investing real money, and since these platforms provide real-time information, you can see your profits or losses in real time. We can say that virtual trading feature is an upgrade to paper trading; traders can however use either of the choices, whatever works for them.

20

~

Changes in India's Derivative Trading Framework

INDIA'S SECURITY MARKET REGULATOR SEBI issued an important circular on 1 October 2024, *"Measures to Strengthen Equity Index Derivatives Framework for Increased Investor Protection and Market Stability"* which can be found at the SEBI website.*

The circular initiated several significant changes to India's derivatives trading framework with the goal of enhancing market stability and investor protection, particularly protection of individual investors.

The key changes and their impact are summarized in this chapter.

Increase in Minimum Contract Size

From 20 November 2024, the lot size for index options, including Nifty options and Bank Nifty options, stand adjusted so as

* https://www.sebi.gov.in/legal/circulars/oct-2024/measures-to-strengthen-equity-index-derivatives-framework-for-increased-investor-protection-and-market-stability_87208.html.

to raise the contract value from the earlier ₹5-10 lakh level to ₹15-20 lakh.

Contract value is calculated as: Strike Price × Lot Size. Considering Nifty had a lot size of 25 prior to 20 November 2024, the contract value of 25000 strike was ₹6,25,000 (25000 × 25).

To increase the contract value, the lot size of Nifty has been increased to 75 to bring it in the range of ₹15-20 lakh (25000 × 75 = ₹18,75,000).

Similar calculation can be done for different indices for the new lot sizes, as displayed in Table 20.1.

Table 20.1

Increase in Contract Values

Index	*Before 20 November 2024*	*New Lot Size After 20 November 2024*
NIFTY	25	75
BANKNIFTY	15	30
FINNIFTY	25	65
MIDCPNIFTY	50	120

This increase in lot size inevitably raises the capital required for of trading, making it harder for smaller retail traders to participate. Thus, individual option buyers have now to pay more given the larger lot and option sellers too have to put up more margin money per lot. This change is intended to limit the participation of small retail investors who may not be able to endure substantial losses.

Upfront Collection of Option Premiums

From 1 February 2025, brokers are mandated to collect option premiums upfront from their clients. This measure is designed to ensure that there is adequate capital to cover ongoing trading positions, thereby reducing the risk of default. This change will mainly affect traders who use brokers that allowed leveraged positions. Discount brokers, such as Zerodha, Upstox already collect full premiums upfront, so this rule may not impact all traders.

Additional Margins on Expiry Day

With effect from 20 November 2024, SEBI has enforced an extra 2% extreme loss margin (ELM) on short options position on expiry days in order to control the heightened volatility typically witnessed on such days. ELM will thus further increase the cost for option sellers.

Prior to 20 November 2024, option sellers needed to deposit margin money when writing or selling contracts. This margin comprised of two components:

1. Initial margin or SPAN margin; and
2. Exposure margin.

Calculation of margin money has been thoroughly explained in my earlier book* but, briefly, initial margin is monitored and collected at the time of placing the sell order while exposure margins may be required over and above the initial margins in order to cover mark-to-market (MTM) losses. MTM or mark-to-market is the daily profit / loss, which is calculated on a day-to-day basis.

Let us now understand the additional ELM, or extreme loss margin, with an example. Suppose you are short on Nifty

---

* *Making Money by Selling Options — Simplified* published by Vision Books (www.visionbooksindia.com). Available at Amazon and Flipkart.

Table 20.2

Margins For an Options Writer after 20 November 2024

Margin	*When They are Applied*
Initial or SPAN Margin	Applied to the option writer (seller) when taking fresh positions.
Exposure Margin	May be applied to the option writer (seller) to cover MTM losses.
ELM (Extreme Loss Margin) NEW: @2% of the Contract Value	Applied to the option writer (seller) on the day of contract expiry.

25000PE expiring on 28 November 2024, having margin requirement of ₹100,000. On the expiry day of this position (28 November) you will have to maintain an additional 2% margin as ELM. This percentage is calculated on the contact value as illustrated below:

Contact value: 25000 (strike) × 25 (lot size) = ₹6,25,000
ELM = 2% × 6,25,000 = ₹12,500.

So on expiry day you now have to a maintain margin of ₹1,12,500, as against the earlier requirement of ₹1 lakh. ELM has been introduced to address the heightened risk associated with selling of option contracts on expiry day.

Table 20.2 summarizes the different margin requirements for an option writer.

Reduction in the Number of Weekly Expiries

After 20 November 2024, there has been considerable changes related to weekly expiries of different Indices. This measure aims to reduce the volatility and speculation linked to weekly expirations and, thus, promote more stable market conditions. Below table summarizes expiry schedule for few indices:

Table 20.3

Expiry Schedule after 20 November 2024

Index	*Weekly Expiry*	*Monthly Expiry*
NIFTY	Thursday of every week	Last Thursday of each month
BANKNIFTY	No weekly expiry	Last Wednesday of each month
FINNIFTY	No weekly expiry	Last Tuesday of each month
MIDCPNIFTY	No weekly expiry	Last Monday of each month

Removal of Calendar Spread Benefits

From 1 February 2025, the margin benefit for calendar spread positions on contract expiry days stands removed. This measure aims to reduce the higher risks associated with expiry days when contract values can vary significantly.

Intraday Monitoring of Position Limits

From 1 April 2025, position limits get monitored intraday, not just at the end of the trading day, in order to prevent excessive risk-taking. SEBI imposed limits on the maximum positions that a single client or broker can hold for a specific contract. Clients are restricted to 5% of the total open interest across all derivative contracts of the same underlying, while brokers are limited to 15%. This measure aims to detect and prevent traders from exceeding allowed limits, thereby reducing the market's systemic risks.

Systemic risk refers to the possibility of a widespread failure within the financial system that can impact all investors, as it jeopardizes the stability of the entire system. A notable example is the 2008 global financial crisis, where the collapse of major institutions like Lehman Brothers affected banks, investors, and the global economy.

Table 20.4

SEBI's New Measures Announced on 1 October 2024

No.	*Measure*	*Effective From*	*Impact on Traders*
1	Increase in Minimum Contract Size	20 November 2024	1. Cost of buying options will rise. 2. Option selling margin will rise. 3. Profit and loss potential will also increase.
2	Upfront Collection of Option Premiums	1 February 2025	Option buyers have to deposit full premium at the time of taking up a making position. Traders using discount brokers will likely not be impacted.
3	ELM — Extreme Loss Margin — additional Margin on Expiry Day	20 November 2024	2% of contract value will be applied as ELM on option writing on the day of expiry. Option sellers will be impacted and they will have to deposit 2% more margin money. ELM will be applied on new and existing, both the positions on expiry day.
4	Reduction in Weekly Expiries	20 November 2024	Fewer weekly contracts to trade for option buyers and sellers.
5	Removal of Calendar Spread Benefits	1 February 2025	Option writers impacted as they will not get hedging benefit and will have to deposit full margin money. Till now, Traders often used to maintain positions across various expiries, known as calendar spreads, which used to offer margin benefits and lower overall margin requirements.
6	Intraday Monitoring of Position Limits	1 April 2025	Retails traders may not be able to reach the positional limits for a contract. Large institutional traders and brokers may be impacted.

Table 20.4 summarizes the impact and schedule of the new measures.

These measures are a part of SEBI's efforts to protect retail investors from substantial losses — and to foster a more stable and transparent market environment. These changes would, however, not have any major impact on the technical aspects of various strategies discussed in this book.

21

~

How to Choose From the 16 Options Trading Strategies

A Ready-Reckoner

TABLE 21.1 SUMMARIZES ALL OUR 16 STRATEGIES discussed in this book along with the conditions in which they are best deployed. Readers can use this table as a ready reckoner for options strategy selection.

In this chapter we have summarized which strategy could be used for different market conditions. I urge readers to go through below mentioned table thoroughly — and use it for a quick reference when initiating new option trades.

Table 21.1

How to Select the Right Strategy — A Ready Reckoner

Strategy Name	*Your Market View*	*Beneficial Price Move*	*Volatility Impact*	*Set-Up*	*Debit / Credit*	*Loss*	*Profit*	*Breakeven Point*	*Stop Trade / Stop Loss / Exit*	*Delta*	*Gamma*	*Vega*	*Theta*	*Comments*
■ Bullish Strategies ■														
Bull Call Spread	Moderately Bullish	Price rises from a certain level.	Benefits from increase in volatility.	2 legs: – Buy ATM CE – Sell OTM CE.	Debit	Fixed, pre-defined.	Fixed, pre-defined.	ATM CE strike *plus* net debit of the strategy.	When 75% of max profit is achieved, or stop loss is hit, or one week before expiry, whichever occurs first.	Positive	Positive	Positive	Negative	
Bull Put Spread	Moderately Bullish	Price stays above a certain level, or rises a bit.	Benefits from reduction in volatility.	2 legs: – Buy OTM PE – Sell ITM PE.	Credit	Fixed, pre-defined.	Fixed, pre-defined.	ITM PE strike *minus* net credit of the strategy.	When 75% of max profit is achieved, or stop loss is hit, or one week before expiry, whichever occurs first.	Positive	Positive	Negative	Positive	This strategy generally has lower upfront cost than the bull call spread.
Call Ratio Back Spread	Bullish	Sharp price rise.	Benefits from increase in volatility.	3 legs: – Sell ITM CE – Buy 2 OTM CEs.	Credit	Fixed; pre-defined.	Big profit potential in case of significant up move.	Two breakeven points: one, if the underlying's price moves down, and another when the price moves up.	When market becomes stagnant and volatility starts falling, or stop loss is hit, or one week before expiry, whichever occurs first.	Positive	Positive	Positive	Generally negative at the start of trade.	

(Contd . . .)

Table 21.1: **How to Select the Right Strategy — A Ready Reckoner** *(. . . contd.)*

Strategy Name	*Your Market View*	*Beneficial Price Move*	*Volatility Impact*	*Set-Up*	*Debit / Credit*	*Loss*	*Profit*	*Breakeven Point*	*Stop Trade / Stop Loss / Exit*	*Delta*	*Gamma*	*Vega*	*Theta*	*Comments*
							■ Bullish Strategies *(. . . contd.)* **■**							
Bear Call Ladder	Very bullish in high volatility market.	Quick price rise.	Increase in volatility is beneficial.	3 legs: – Sell ITM CE – Buy ATM CE – Buy OTM CE.	Credit	Fixed; pre-defined.	Big profit potential in case of significant up move.	Two breakeven points; one, if the underlying's price moves down, and second when the price moves up.	When market becomes stagnant and volatility falls; or if stop loss is hit; or one week before expiry; whichever occurs first.	Positive	Positive	Positive	Generally negative at the start of trade.	This strategy is an enhancement of call ratio back spread and should be used when volatility is very high.
							■ Bearish Strategies ■							
Bear Call Spread	Moderately bearish.	Fall in price.	Benefits from reduction in volatility.	2 legs: – Buy OTM CE – Sell ITM CE.	Credit	Fixed; pre-defined.	Fixed; pre-defined.	ITM strike *plus* net credit of the strategy.	When 75% of max profit is achieved; or stop loss is hit; or one week before expiry; whichever occurs first.	Negative	Mixed	Negative	Positive	
Bear Put Spread	Moderately bearish	Fall in price.	Increase in volatility is beneficial.	2 legs: – Buy ITM PE – Sell OTM PE.	Debit	Fixed; pre-defined.	Fixed, pre-defined.	ITM strike *minus* net debit of the strategy.	When 75% of max profit is achieved; or stop loss is hit; or one week before expiry; whichever occurs first.	Negative	Positive	Positive	Negative	
Put Ratio Back Spread	Bearish	Quick fall in price.	Benefits from reduction in volatility.	3 legs: – Sell ITM PE – Buy 2 OTM PE.	Credit	Fixed, pre-defined.	Big profit potential if the fall in price is significant.	Two breakeven points; one, if the underlying's price moves down, and second when the price moves up.	When price becomes stagnant and it might reverse; or stop loss is hit; or one week before expiry; whichever occurs first.	Depends on the ratio of short and long puts.	Mixed	Negative	Positive	

(Contd . . .)

Table 21.1: **How to Select the Right Strategy — A Ready Reckoner** *(. . . contd.)*

Strategy Name	*Your Market View*	*Beneficial Price Move*	*Volatility Impact*	*Set-Up*	*Debit / Credit*	*Loss*	*Profit*	*Breakeven Point*	*Stop Trade / Stop Loss / Exit*	*Delta*	*Gamma*	*Vega*	*Theta*	*Comments*
■ **Bearish Strategies** *(. . . contd.)* ■														
Bull Put Ladder	Very bearish	Quick fall in price.	Benefits from reduction in volatility.	3 legs: – Sell ITM PE – Buy ATM PE – Buy OTM PE.	Credit	Fixed, pre-defined.	Big profit potential if the price fall is significant.	Two breakeven points; one, if the underlying's price moves down, and another when the price moves up.	When market becomes stagnant and may possibly reverse; or stop loss is hit; or one week before expiry; whichever occurs first.	Depends on the ratio of short puts to long puts.	Depends on the ratio of short puts to long puts.	Negative	Positive	This strategy is an enhancement of put ratio back spread and should be used when you are very confidant that market will move down from its current levels.
■ **Neutral / Range bound / Sideways Strategies** ■														
Long Straddle	Market will be range bound.	Quick, big price move in either direction.	Increase in volatility is beneficial.	2 legs: – Buy ATM CE – Buy ATM PE.	Debit	Fixed, pre-defined.	Variable gains. Big gains if price moves significantly in either direction.	Two breakeven points: one, if the underlying's price moves down, and another when the price moves up.	When market becomes stagnant and volatility is falling; or with the stop loss is hit; or one week before expiry; whichever occurs first.	Neutral Delta.	High positive gamma.	High positive Vega	High negative theta.	
Short Straddle	Market will be range bound.	Price remains range bound.	Benefits from reduction in volatility.	2 legs: – Sell ATM CE – Sell ATM PE	Credit	Potentially unlimited in case of a big price move in either direction.	Limited profit potential.	Two breakeven points: one, if the underlying's price moves down, and another when the price moves up.	When market starts trending in either direction and volatility rises; or when stop loss is hit; or one week before expiry; whichever occurs first.	Neutral Delta.	High negative Gamma	Relatively high negative Vega	High positive Theta	

(Contd . . .)

Table 21.1: **How to Select the Right Strategy — A Ready Reckoner** *(. . . contd.)*

Strategy Name	*Your Market View*	*Beneficial Price Move*	*Volatility Impact*	*Set-Up*	*Debit / Credit*	*Loss*	*Profit*	*Breakeven Point*	*Stop Trade / Stop Loss / Exit*	*Delta*	*Gamma*	*Vega*	*Theta*	*Comments*
■ Neutral / Range bound / Sideways Strategies *(. . . contd.)* **■**														
Long Strangle	Market will be range bound.	Big price move in either direction.	Benefits from increase in volatility.	2 legs: – Buy OTM CE – Buy OTM PE.	Debit	Limited loss	Potential of unlimited profit if price moves significantly in either direction.	Two breakeven points: one, if the underlying's price moves down, and another when the underlying's price moves up.	When market becomes stagnant and volatility falls, or when stop loss is hit; or one week before expiry; whichever occurs first.	Neutral Delta.	High positive gamma.	High overall positive Vega.	Relatively high negative Theta.	This strategy is cheaper to implement than the long straddle.
Short Strangle	Market will be range bound.	Price remaining range bound.	Benefits from a reduction in volatility.	2 legs: – Sell OTM CE – Sell OTM PE.	Credit	Potentially unlimited loss in case of a big price move in either direction.	Limited profit potential.	Two breakeven points: one, if the underlying's price moves down, and another when the price moves up.	When market starts trending in either direction and volatility increases; or stop loss is hit; or one week before expiry; whichever occurs first.	Neutral Delta.	High negative Gamma	Relatively high negative Vega	Relatively high positive Theta.	This strategy is cheaper to implement than the short straddle.
Iron Butterfly	Market will be range bound.	Price remaining range bound.	Benefits from a reduction in volatility.	4 legs: – Sell ATM CE – Sell ATM PE – Buy OTM CE – Buy OTM PE.	Credit	Limited, predefined loss.	Limited and predefined profit.	Two breakeven points: one, if the underlying's price moves down; and another when the underlying's price moves up.	When 75% of max profit is achieved, or when the stop loss is hit; or one week before expiry; whichever occurs first.	Neutral Delta.	Overall negative Gamma.	Over all negative Vega.	Overall positive Theta.	This strategy is a combination of short straddle and long strangle.

(Contd . . .)

Table 21.1: **How to Select the Right Strategy — A Ready Reckoner** *(. . . contd.)*

Strategy Name	*Your Market View*	*Beneficial Price Move*	*Volatility Impact*	*Set-Up*	*Debit / Credit*	*Loss*	*Profit*	*Breakeven Point*	*Stop Trade / Stop Loss / Exit*	*Delta*	*Gamma*	*Vega*	*Theta*	*Comments*
■ **Neutral / Range bound / Sideways Strategies** *(. . . contd.)* ■														
Iron Condor	Market will be range bound.	Price remains range bound.	Benefits from fall in volatility.	4 legs: – Sell OTM CE – Sell OTM PE – Buy further OTM CE – Buy further OTM PE.	Credit	Limited, pre-defined loss.	Limited and pre-defined profit.	Two breakeven points; one, if the underlying's price moves down, and another when the price moves up.	When 75% of max profit is achieved, or the stop loss is hit, or one week before expiry; whichever occurs first.	Neutral Delta.	Overall negative Gamma.	Over all negative Vega.	Overall positive Theta.	This strategy is a combination of short strangle and long strangle and is cheaper to implement than the iron butterfly.
■ **Hedging Strategies** ■														
Synthetic call option	Bullish	Price rise will benefit the strategy.	Benefits from increase in volatility.	2 legs: – Buy futures or stocks – Buy ATM PE.	Debit	Limited, pre-defined loss.	Big profit potential in case of significant up move.	Futures or stock's price, *plus* the premium paid for the ATM put option.	Continue to hold futures / stock position if prices go down, since losses will be covered by the ATM PE.	Positive	Positive	Positive	Negative	This is basically a hedging strategy to protect long positions.
Synthetic put option	Bearish	Price fall will benefit the strategy.	Benefits from increase in volatility.	2 legs: – Sell futures – Buy ATM CE.	Debit	Limited, pre-defined loss.	Big profit potential with significant down move.	Futures price *minus* the premium paid for buying the ATM call option.	Continue to short futures position if prices go up, since losses will be covered by ATM CE.	Negative	Positive	Positive	Negative	This is basically a hedging strategy to protect short positions.

22

~

Epilogue

WE HAVE NOW COME TO THE END OF THIS BOOK. I have tried to write a comprehensive guide that equips you for the world of option trading, and the knowledge and strategies needed to navigate the complex landscape of financial derivatives.

We started by looking at the fundamental concepts of options, including their types, terminology, and basic mechanics.

We then progressed to more advanced sections, exploring various trading strategies that can be employed to manage risk and enhance profitability. These strategies encompass bullish, bearish and neutral market scenarios along with hedging strategies, enabling readers to adapt their approach to different market conditions.

We also highlighted the importance of understanding option Greeks, which are key factors that influence option pricing and behaviour. By acquiring a sound understanding of Greeks, you would be able to better assess risk, calculate potential returns, and make informed decisions based on market analysis.

Whether you are a novice or an experienced trader, this book offers well-rounded knowledge and guidance on options, covering topics from basic concepts to advanced strategies. I hope that at the end of this book, you would have a solid foundation to approach options trading with confidence and a strategic mindset.

All the best!